Foreign Exchange Rates

Predicting foreign exchange rates has presented a long-standing challenge for economists. However, the recent advances in computational techniques, statistical methods, newer datasets on emerging market currencies, etc., offer some hope. While we are still unable to beat a driftless random walk model, there has been serious progress in the field. This book provides an in-depth assessment of the use of novel statistical approaches and machine learning tools in predicting foreign exchange rate movement.

First, it offers a historical account of how exchange rate regimes have evolved over time, which is critical to understanding turning points in a historical time series. It then presents an overview of the previous attempts at modeling exchange rates, and how different methods fared during this process. At the core sections of the book, the author examines the time series characteristics of exchange rates and how contemporary statistics and machine learning can be useful in improving predictive power, compared to previous methods used.

Exchange rate determination is an active research area, and this book will appeal to graduate-level students of international economics, international finance, open economy macroeconomics, and management. The book is written in a clear, engaging, and straightforward way, and will greatly improve access to this much-needed knowledge in the field.

Arif Orçun Söylemez is Associate Professor at the Economics Department of Marmara University, Istanbul, Turkey.

Routledge Focus on Economics and Finance

The fields of economics are constantly expanding and evolving. This growth presents challenges for readers trying to keep up with the latest important insights. Routledge Focus on Economics and Finance presents short books on the latest big topics, linking in with the most cutting-edge economics research.

Individually, each title in the series provides coverage of a key academic topic, whilst collectively the series forms a comprehensive collection across the whole spectrum of economics.

For more information about this series, please visit www.routledge.com/Routledge-Focus-on-Economics-and-Finance/book-series/RFEF

Foreign Exchange Rates

A Research Overview of the Latest
Prediction Techniques

Arif Orçun Söylemez

Routledge
Taylor & Francis Group

LONDON AND NEW YORK

First published 2021
by Routledge
2 Park Square, Milton Park, Abingdon, Oxon OX14 4RN

and by Routledge
52 Vanderbilt Avenue, New York, NY 10017

Routledge is an imprint of the Taylor & Francis Group, an informa business

British Library Cataloguing-in-Publication Data
A catalogue record for this book is available from the British Library

Library of Congress Cataloging-in-Publication Data
Names: Söylemez, Arif Orçun, author.
Title: Foreign exchange rates : a research overview of the latest
    prediction techniques / Arif Orçun Söylemez.
Description: Abingdon, Oxon ; New York, NY : Routledge, 2021. |
    Series: Routledge focus on economics and finance | Includes
    bibliographical references and index.
Identifiers: LCCN 2020043741 (print) | LCCN 2020043742 (ebook) |
    ISBN 9780367609917 (hbk) | ISBN 9781003102809 (ebk)
Subjects: LCSH: Foreign exchange rates—Econometric models. | Foreign
    exchange market. | International finance.
Classification: LCC HG3851 .S67 2021 (print) | LCC HG3851 (ebook) |
    DDC 332.4/5610112—dc23
LC record available at https://lccn.loc.gov/2020043741
LC ebook record available at https://lccn.loc.gov/2020043742

ISBN: 978-0-367-60991-7 (hbk)
ISBN: 978-1-003-10280-9 (ebk)

Typeset in Times New Roman
by Apex CoVantage, LLC

Access the Support Material: www.routledge.com/9780367609917

To my mom, Gülseren Söylemez,
and to my late father, Nazmi Söylemez,
for all the good memories with them . . .

Contents

Figures

Tables

Preface

The global foreign exchange market is indisputably the largest market in the world with an average daily trading volume of $6.6 trillion, according to the latest 2019 Triennial Central Bank Survey of the Bank for International Settlements (BIS).* In addition to its being the largest market, it is also one of the most problematic markets for economists and policymakers. It is problematic because the discipline of economics has been unsuccessful virtually in every attempt to explain the future exchange rate movements to date. In short, exchange rate movements are yet to be explained. This situation of lack of a stable and reliable pricing model for the exchange rates is simply known as the '*exchange rate determination problem.*'

In 1983, Kenneth Rogoff – from US Federal Reserve (FED) – and Richard Meese – from the University of California at Berkeley – have shown how severe a drawback this particular problem is with a seminal paper they have written. In that famous 1983 paper, Meese and Rogoff have tested the predictive powers of a set of popular structural and time series exchange rate models of the time against that of a driftless random walk process. Quite shockingly, the random walk process has beaten all the structural models with its better out-of-sample forecasting accuracy. This is a shocking finding because, from a purely statistical point of view, the random walk processes are the discrete-time counterparts of the continuous Brownian motion processes. As well known, the Brownian motion processes cannot be predicted whatsoever. In plain English, this means that the most powerful forecast model of the exchange rates according to this seminal paper was not a forecast model itself. Since then, myriad empirical

---

* Daily $6.6 trillion trading volume on average is the turnover of all the OTC foreign exchange products on a net-to-net basis. The included OTC products are the spot transactions, outright forwards, foreign exchange swaps, currency swaps, and FX options. Detailed data (such as the break-down of this figure by each product, by country, by counterparty of the transactions or by currency type) could be found on the following URL from the BIS webpage: https://stats.bis.org/statx/srs/table/d11.1

studies have hopelessly tried to reverse this absurd and gloomy finding of Rogoff and Meese only to observe over and over again that the random walk model is indeed the unrivaled champion of the foreign exchange forecasting business. I hope that you have now understood what I was trying to express when I said that the global foreign exchange rates market is one of the most problematic markets in the world for policymakers. It is problematic (and scary) because it is huge and we do not have a clue for predicting where the foreign exchange rates may go in the future.

From the economists' standpoint, the issue is even more nerve-wracking and complicated. First of all, economists by their profession are the very people who are expected to model the dynamic behavior of the exchange rates. But this task is easier said than done due to various complexities repeatedly observed in the foreign exchange datasets. Take, for example, the '*exchange rate disconnect puzzle.*' According to this well-known problem, exchange rates typically produce highly volatile time series. Macroeconomic variables, on the other hand, are usually significantly less volatile than the exchange rates. This sort of a volatility mismatch can lead to an important and hard-to-overcome technical complexity because when one attempts to explain the exchange rates using macroeconomic variables such as the inflation rates, interest rates, growth rates, etc., as explanatory variables, those variables can hardly do a good job of explaining the variations in the exchange rates since they, themselves, do not vary at the same rate (to be more precise, that volatility difference would be an issue whenever the frequencies of the time series in the frequency domain do not match; models using economic variables could still be made consistent with the excess volatility of exchange rates as long as the log differences of the fundamentals follow persistent stationary processes in the time domain or their frequencies match with that of the exchange rates in the frequency domain). In short, the classical simple regression techniques, only based on the simple traditional assumption of the superiority of the BLUE (best linear unbiased) estimators, used to explain/predict the exchange rate movements, would require the satisfaction of a few more issues, and if these points are not met (and usually they are not met), our simple linear regression models would be doomed to fail in returning satisfactorily high coefficient of determination values. Without further boring the reader with technical issues, let me put it in this way – economists face two difficulties: i) they need to model the exchange rate movements, and ii) in that effort, they have to invent new and ingenious quantitative models.

I hope that I have set the tone for the rest of this book with these prefatory notes. This book is about exchange rates. To be more specific, however, it aims to revisit the long-standing exchange rate determination problem and put it to the test with more recent statistical and data science techniques in order to see whether we can improve the forecasting power of our traditional structural models (i.e. models using economic variables to explain the foreign exchange rate movements) with the help of these contemporary techniques.

That is why I do not intend to lose much time and energy with an introduction of the foreign exchange rate market. That said, I will nevertheless begin with a concise discussion of the exchange rate market, focusing on the post-World War II era. I will stretch this concise summary of the market starting from 1944 to the present time, hoping that this brief discussion will highlight some of the important turning points in the global foreign exchange market.

Second and more importantly, I will focus on the structural models of exchange rate determination. In the subsequent chapters, I will introduce some nonlinear regime-switching models, along with some simple supervised machine learning algorithms. I will, of course, use all of these techniques on a real dataset in this book in order to show their applications using computer programs and software. These exercises on a real dataset will also allow us to see whether it is possible to improve our predictions using these techniques or not. I will make an overall assessment in the final part of the book.

Since I have introduced my book, I now would like to extend my most sincere gratitude to some people, without the support of whom this book could not have been written. First and foremost, I want to thank Prof. Jun Jongbyun of Suffolk University, for he has been such a good and patient teacher to me for so many years. For useful comments and moral support, I want to thank Prof. Sadullah Çelik from Marmara University. One of the persons who deserve to be thanked at the highest possible level with regard to this particular book is Kristina Abbots, my editor, who has always been helpful to me as I was planning, writing, and finally submitting this book. Last but not least, I cannot thank my mom enough for her patience and never-ending support to me in this life. Needless to say, the usual disclaimers apply.

Arif Orçun Söylemez
August 2020

1 A brief introduction of the global foreign exchange market

As World War II (WWII) was approaching to its end in 1944, the US and its allies came together in the town of Bretton Woods in New Hampshire, USA, for an important conference, whose official name was the United Nations Monetary and Financial Conference. As this official name suggested, the 730 delegates representing all the 44 Allied nations in this gathering were trying to agree upon the global monetary and financial rules that were to be established right after the war. This important gathering would later come to be called the Bretton Woods Conference for the understandable reason, and the international financial system that it gave rise to in the aftermath of the war would be known as the Bretton Woods system.

As for the delegates, they made some highly significant decisions during the conference. For example, they agreed upon the necessity of establishing two important international organizations after the war, both of which would play highly pivotal roles in the construction of the post-WWII global economic and financial architecture. These two institutions were the International Monetary Fund (IMF) and the International Bank for Reconstruction and Development (IBRD, also known as the World Bank).

If we focus on understanding the true meaning of the post-WWII economic and financial activities of the Allied nations (or you may choose to say the countries of the whole Western Bloc), it is clear that these nations were in search of an economically and financially intertwined world, where the economic benefits of countries would be interlinked. The main driver behind this motive of them for redesigning an economically and financially connected world is very understandable from a classical liberal point of view: If the welfare of countries became mutually dependent, according to the classical thinkers, countries would never seek a war again in order not to jeopardize their own economic welfare.[1] Based on this sort of a classical liberal perspective of 'perpetual peace,' boosting the free international trade was at the top of the to-do-list of the Western countries in the post-WWII world.

Once we approach the decisions taken at the Bretton Woods Conference from such an angle of peace and stability-seeking, we can see the complementarity between the decisions more easily. For example, the World Bank – as a bank for reconstruction and development, as its full official name suggested – was much needed because the war-torn infrastructure had to be fixed immediately in order to integrate the countries into the global production nets. Those countries would be able to trade with each other only if they have produced something tradable. If the logic behind the establishment of the World Bank is clear, let us now turn to the role of the IMF. First of all, it is not surprising to see that the IMF's mandate was to facilitate the expansion and balanced growth of international trade.[2] Obviously, the Western countries were trying to minimize the risk of another episode of a destructive war in the future through weaving a robust cobweb of trade linkages among countries. One of the threats to the sustainability of international trade was the risk of financial collapse. Consider for a moment that countries A, B, and C are trading with each other and A is a net importer of B's goods, while B is a net importer of C's goods. What happens if A collapses for any reason, say due to the faulty decisions of the policymakers or simply due to an earthquake, etc.? A cannot pay for the goods it has purchased from B and so B may fail in honoring its payments to C. In a domino effect, the collapse of A spreads to other nations, and this may give world trade some bitter blows. The IMF, whose mandate was to make sure that the international trade would expand, was therefore established as a lender of last resort to countries like A in this example – i.e. to the countries that could spark a global meltdown of trade.

In addition to their decisions to establish the World Bank and the IMF, the Allied nations had also agreed upon an exchange rate standard whereby the value of the US Dollar would be fixed to gold and the values of the major currencies would be pegged to that of the US Dollar. This was a gold standard in disguise. Without any doubt, this sort of an internationally accepted fixed exchange rate regime had the capacity to serve as an effective tool to strip the exchange rate risk off the international transactions. Therefore, it should be seen probably as the most critical and essential step toward boosting free trade among Western countries.

Although the idea of achieving perpetual peace on earth using free international trade was an ingenious dream of the Western countries imminently following the end of WWII, some of the tools of this classical liberal perpetual peace idea lost their allure over the years. The gold standard of the Bretton Woods system, for instance, would stay in effect until 1971, when it was discarded by the US when the administration of President Richard M. Nixon, faced with economic and political hardships, decided to opt out and a set of leading nations, including the UK and France, hopped onto the same wagon with the US out of their desire to regain power in the design of their own domestic monetary policies.

After the dismissal of the Bretton Woods system of exchange rates, the world entered into a new phase. Exchange rates between an increasing number of currencies started to be determined freely by the interaction of the demand and supply forces in the market. Therefore, we can claim that this new era was, in fact, an era of floating exchange rates. In this new era, finding the right specification of the economic/econometric models for better predicting the future exchange rates became an active field of research in the literature. From the early 1970s to 1983, economists had identified various macroeconomic variables that could be used to make exchange rate predictions until Rogoff and Meese showed in 1983 the uselessness of the various structural models – which were relying on these variables – against a driftless random walk.

Let us articulate what Meese and Rogoff did in 1983 and how they arrived at their gloomy finding, which is a finding that is still empirically valid after all those years, and which is a finding that also serves as the very cause for the existence of this book. In a seminal paper they wrote in the *Journal of International Economics*, Meese and Rogoff compared the out-of-sample forecasting powers of the six popular structural and time series models of exchange rates using the data for Dollar/Pound, Dollar/German Mark, Dollar/Yen, and trade-weighted Dollar exchange rates. The structural models they employed were the flexible-price (Frenkel-Bilson) and sticky-price (Dornbusch-Frankel) monetary models along with a sticky-price model augmented with the current account (Hooper-Morton).

The most general specification, covering all these three structural models, was as follows:

$$s = a_0 + a_1\left(m - m^*\right) + a_2\left(y - y^*\right) + a_3\left(r_s - r_s^*\right) + a_4\left(\pi^e - \pi^{e*}\right)$$
$$+ a_5\overline{TB} + a_6\overline{TB}^* + u, \tag{1}$$

where the regressand, s, stood for the log value of the Dollar price of the foreign currency. As for the regressors, $m - m^*$ stood for the log differences in the money supplies between the US and the foreign country. By the way, the asterisk signs on top of some variables were to indicate that these were the foreign country observations of that variable. Similarly, $y - y^*$ stood for the log value differences in the growth rates of the US and the foreign country. $r_s - r_s^*$ and $\pi^e - \pi^{e*}$ were the differences in the non-log-transformed values of the short-run interest rates and the expected inflation rates in the US and the foreign country, respectively. $\overline{TB}$ showed cumulated trade balance of the US and $\overline{TB}^*$ was its counterpart for the foreign country. The disturbance term of this stochastic model was u.

Eq. (1) was the most general specification combining all the three structural models since the model in (1) was boiling down to the Frenkel-Bilson model once the researcher set a_4, a_5, and a_6 equal to zero. By the way, we will reproduce this model from scratch in the following chapter as we talk about the monetary model of exchange rates. Similarly, the researcher could set only a_5 and a_6 equal to zero and then Eq. (1) would become the Dornbusch-Frenkel model. Eq. (1) itself, with none of the coefficients constrained to be zero, is the Hooper-Morton model.

Apart from these three structural models, Meese and Rogoff tested univariate and multivariate time series models as well. They employed a long AR model where the longest lag (M) they considered was based on a function of sample size, i.e. $M = N/logN$. As the multivariate model, they employed the AR terms along with lagged values of the structural variables in Eq. (1). Using the mean squared prediction error (MSPE) and mean absolute error (MAE) from the out-of-sample forecasts as the model selection criteria, Meese and Rogoff chose a driftless random walk model as the best predictor above all the structural and time series models they tried. That was a shocking finding simply because random walk models cannot be predicted. In order to understand why it is impossible to predict the random walk processes, let us look at the driftless random walk model that was used in the paper of Meese and Rogoff:

$$s_{t+1} = s_t + \varepsilon_{t+1}$$

where s_{t+1} and s_t are the exchange rates at time $t + 1$ and t, respectively, and ε_{t+1} is nothing but a white noise error term with a central value of zero and time-invariant variance (i.e. $\varepsilon_{t+1} \sim [0, \sigma]$). If we make a prediction at time t for the exchange rate that is likely to occur at time $t + 1$, we encounter the following absurd result.

$$E_t(s_{t+1}) = E_t(s_t) + E_t(\varepsilon_{t+1}) = s_t$$

In the preceding notation, $E_t(\varepsilon_{t+1})$ becomes equal to zero and goes away since we assumed $\varepsilon_{t+1} \sim (0, \sigma)$, i.e. economic agents – either because they form their expectations rationally or adaptively – do not make systematic mistakes. $E_t(s_t)$ is equal to s_t because s_t is known at time t and therefore we do not need to expect a value for it – it is given. In sum, $E_t(s_t) + E_t(\varepsilon_{t+1}) = s_t + 0 = E_t(s_{t+1})$ and that is why the expected value of tomorrow's exchange rate is equal to the current exchange rate. In sum, the best prediction is to take the last closing value of the exchange rate and use it as our best estimate for the future. As if this is not disappointing enough, there are other problems of using a random walk model for predictions. Remember that we said $E_t(\varepsilon_{t+1})$ becomes equal to zero and goes away. But this is the expected value of the error. In reality, however, the error can be a negative or a positive value, as well (after all it is centrally distributed around zero with the non-zero variation of σ in both directions); the random walk only tells us that the most likely value of the exchange rate tomorrow is the current value of the exchange rate, but there is some non-negligible chance that the realized value of the exchange rate tomorrow can exceed the current value and there is also some non-negligible chance that the realized value of the exchange rate tomorrow can be lower than the current value. There is no useful information in this prediction, as you see. Anyone could tell the same outcome without bothering herself with mathematical models. There is simply (and sadly) no new information in saying that tomorrow the exchange rate is either going to be higher than today's exchange rate or be equal to it or be lower than it; these are the all possibilities, anyway.

To wrap up the discussion so far, the global foreign exchange (FX) market is huge. The daily cross-border turnover on average in this market is estimated to linger around $6.6 trillion by the Bank for International Settlements (BIS). That figure is more than enough to give currencies the top spot as the most widely traded asset class in the global financial markets. Yet there exists no known economic/econometric model that one could rely on in order to predict the future movements of exchange rates. As you can tell, this is analogous to saying that we do not have any reliable asset-pricing model for the most popular financial asset in the world.

Notes

1 Democracy and free trade, according to classical liberals, would reduce the incidence of wars (see O'neal et al. (1996) for further discussion and testing of that view). www.jstor.org/stable/425131?seq=1
2 For better insight about the objectives of the International Monetary Fund, see the following link: www.imf.org/en/About/Factsheets/The-IMF-and-the-World-Trade-Organization

2 Prominent structural models for exchange rate determination

The preceding chapter was about the ineffectiveness of the structural models in predicting the exchange rates. I, nonetheless, would like to devote this chapter to constructing some of the most prominent structural models from scratch, for I believe this is a required exercise due to the simple reason that we can understand the critical issues hidden in these models only as we develop them.

Interest parity rules

Since we are going to develop the models, I prefer moving forward with a simple exercise. Let us begin by assuming that we have $1 in our pocket. Let us further assume that we can effortlessly use this money either to invest in the US market or in the UK market. Again, by assumption, let both the US and UK markets offer the same financial assets. Additionally, say that these two countries have comparable sovereign risk ratings. Finally, assume that we are rational.

Those being our assumptions, say 1 Pound today buys S Dollars (i.e. £1 = $S at the spot market) and we plan to invest our money in a one-week repo instrument. Let the weekly repo yields in the US be 'i' and in the UK 'i^*.' Our money would become $(1 + i)$ if we invested in the US repo market, and it would become £$(1 + i^*)/S$ if we invested in the UK repo market.

Because there cannot be long-lasting arbitrage opportunities in the financial markets, these two gains should be equivalent to each other: $(1 + i) \equiv$ £$(1 + i^*)/S$. Beware that the right hand side (RHS) and left hand side (LHS) sums are expressed in different currencies. Let us now try to express both sides of the equivalence in the same currency, for instance in Dollars. In order to do that, we have to convert £$(1 + i^*)/S$ into its US Dollar worth using the exchange rate that is happening one week later. Let the exchange rate after one week be £1 = $F. Then, £$(1 + i^*)/S \equiv $(1 + i^*)F/S$. Now we can write $\$(1 + i) = \$(1 + i^*)F/S$. For the sake of easier handling, let us log linearize this equality as follows:

$$ln(1+i) = ln(1+i^*)F/S$$

Using the logarithmic rules, we can rewrite the preceding notation as follows:[1]

$$i = i^* + f - s,$$

where f and s are the log values of the forward and spot exchange rates. Please note that i and i^* are not log-transformed. I would like to focus a little bit on the meaning of $f - s$ before moving on. *First of all, recall that $f - s = ln(F/S)$.* We can add $(+S - S)$, which is zero, to the RHS of this equation to end up with the following notation.

$$
\begin{aligned}
f - s &= ln\left(\frac{F - S + S}{S}\right) = ln\left(1 + \frac{F - S}{S}\right) \\
&= \frac{F - S}{S} = \text{'percentage change in the exchange rates'}
\end{aligned}
$$

That is why we can conclude that the percentage change in the exchange rates is equal to the differences in the yields, or the interest rates.

$$f - s = \Delta s_{t+1} = i - i^* \tag{2}$$

where $\Delta s_{t+1} = s_{t+1} - s_t.$[2]

The linear model presented by Eq. (2) sets forward an interest parity rule. That rule relates the percentage changes in the exchange rates to interest rate (or yield) differentials of comparable assets in different countries. If f, i.e. the forward rate, is hedged, then the rule in Eq. (2) is called the covered interest parity rule, while it is called the uncovered interest parity rule if forward exchange rate f is unhedged.

Purchasing power parity rule

The international Fisher Equation is a good departure point to start constructing the purchasing power parity (PPP) rule. According to the reputed Fisher equation, nominal interest rates reflect the sum of the real interest rates and the expected inflation rates. The International Fisher Equation is nothing but its extension to two countries:

$$i = r + \Delta p_{t+1}^{e} \quad \text{(Fisher equation for home country)}$$
$$i^* = r^* + \Delta p_{t+1}^{e^*} \quad \text{(Fisher equation for foreign country)}$$

In these notations, r stands for the real interest rate at home, while r^* is its foreign country counterpart. Δp_{t+1}^{e}, on the other hand, is equal to the log differences in the expected and current price levels at home between time $t + 1$ and time t. $\Delta p_{t+1}^{e^*}$ is its foreign country counterpart.

If we deduct the foreign country Fisher equation from the home country equation, we end up with the following International Fisher Equation:

$$i - i^* = (r - r^*) + \left(\Delta p_{t+1}^{e} - \Delta p_{t+1}^{e^*} \right) \quad \text{(International Fisher equation)}$$

The real interest rate differential, i.e. $(r - r^*)$ in the preceding notation, should boil down to zero if international capital is allowed to move freely across the borders. Considering the mass movement of countries toward financial liberalization since the early 1980s, we can claim that in a liberal international financial setting the following should hold:

$$i - i^* = \left(\Delta p_{t+1}^{e} - \Delta p_{t+1}^{e^*} \right) \quad \text{(International Fisher Eq. with freely moving}$$
international capital)

Since $i - i^* = \Delta s_{t+1}$, we can rewrite the International Fisher Eq. with freely moving international capital as follows:

$$\Delta s_{t+1} = \left(\Delta p_{t+1}^{e} - \Delta p_{t+1}^{e^*} \right) \quad (3)$$

Eq. (3) is known as the PPP rule. In plain English, what PPP says is that the percentage change in exchange rates should be equal to the expected inflation rate differential between countries.

Monetary model of exchange rates

We have seen two of the main exchange rate models so far, i.e.: i) the interest parity rule, and ii) the purchasing power parity rule of exchange rates. The interest parity rule is a direct result of the assumption of 'no-financial arbitrage.' Recall that the interest parity rule was the outcome of our efforts to match the yields of two similar financial portfolios in two different countries, the US and the UK.

The idea behind the purchasing power parity, however, could be attributable to the assumption of 'no-arbitrage in the trading of real commodities,' since PPP was adjusting the exchange rates in such a manner that the inflation differences (and domestic price differences as a result) were automatically swept away by the changes in exchange rates.

The assumption of no-arbitrage, whether it be in the financial market or be in the goods market, is a very strong assumption of free market economics. But this time, I want to focus on another strong assumption of classical economics which similarly rests at the heart of free market thinking. This strong assumption that I am talking about is the tendency of the markets to come to an equilibrium. According to the classical economists and the proponents of the free market ideal, markets have an innate tendency to equilibrate the forces of supply and demand. If that is true, the equilibrium exchange rate would occur at the point where the money supply becomes equal to the money demand.

Let us say M/P is the money supply in the home country and M^*/P^* is the money supply in the foreign country. Money demand, on the other hand, is a function of liquidity preference, i.e. L^d, which itself is a function of interest rate (i) and the income (Y). In the equilibrium, then, we must have the following equality for the home country: $M/P = i^{-\lambda}Y^\beta$, where $-\lambda$ is a negative number indicating that people demand less cash when the yields rise and β is a positive number indicating that people demand more cash when their incomes rise. For the sake of easiness and without loss of generality, let us assume that λ and β are the same across the countries; then we can write the following for the foreign country: $M^*/P^* = i^{*-\lambda}Y^{*\beta}$. Again for the sake of easiness and without loss of generality, let us equate λ to its numeraire value so we work with $M/P = i^{-1}Y^\beta$, which will give us the same information in a much more neat way. If we log linearize these two equilibria, we end up with the following equations:

$$m - p = -i + \beta y \quad \text{(Equilibrium condition in the home country)}$$
$$m^* - p^* = -i^* + \beta y^* \quad \text{(Equilibrium condition in the foreign country)}$$

Rearranging these two equilibria provides us with the following equation:

$$i - i^* = \beta(y - y^*) - (m - m^*) + (p - p^*)$$

We already know from our earlier discussions that $i - i^* = \Delta s_{t+1}$. So, if we replace the LHS of the preceding notation with Δs_{t+1}, we end up with the following monetary model of exchange rates:

$$\Delta s_{t+1} = \beta(y - y^*) - (m - m^*) + (p - p^*)$$

Asset-pricing approach to exchange rate determination

Michael Mussa integrated the very idea of asset pricing to the above model in 1982 and started an energetic line of research in the field of exchange rate economics. Asset prices reflect not only the current situation, but also the expectations. Take for example the discounted cash flows (DCF) model of company valuation. In the DCF model, the value of a company depends on the present values of all the cash flows in the future. Likewise, the fair value of a bond is equal to the discounted value of the face value of the paper at maturity and the discounted values of all its coupons if it is a coupon-bearing bond. Whatever the underlying asset is, if we are to find the fair value of it, we first need to estimate the future cash flows due to the asset and then discount them properly and sum them up. Mussa implemented this simple idea to the exchange rates, assuming that the currency is an asset itself from a financial point of view and constructed the following model of exchange rates:

$$\Delta s_{t+1} = \sum_{t=0}^{n} \beta^{t+1} (y^e - y^{e*})_t - \sum_{t=0}^{n} [(m^e - m^{e*})_t + (p^e - p^{e*})_t],$$

where n is the foreseeable time horizon, for which the investors do have a hunch. Beyond n, it is almost impossible for them to make learned guesses – that is to say, their information set contains information that is relevant for n periods.

As you see, according to this model, exchange rates do not only depend on the contemporary differences between the growth rates, money supplies, and price levels of countries, but also depend on the expectations of investors for them for the next n periods.

Once we incorporate trade balance data into the monetary model, we obtain a modified form of the Hooper-Morton model adjusted under the asset-pricing approach. Recall that the Hooper-Morton model had the most general specification in Meese and Rogoff's 1983 paper and it was presented by Eq. (1) in the previous chapter.

A common problem of the models

A careful eye must have already caught the trick in all these very essential models of exchange rate determination, all of which are based on very strong and undeniable assumptions of economics and finance, such as the rule of no long-lasting arbitrage or the tendency of freely functioning markets toward reaching an equilibrium. The trick is that all these models are dependent on the relationship between the interest (yield) differences between countries and the exchange rate of the currencies of these countries. In other words, the interest parity rule – especially the uncovered one for predicting the path of exchange rates in freely floating exchange rate regimes – serves as the backbone of all of these models. If the relationship between the interest rate differences and the exchange rates do not hold, then neither PPP nor the other models hold. That is why I want to concentrate on the uncovered interest parity (UIP) rule in more detail. Recall that we expressed the UIP rule as follows:

$$f - s_t = i - i^*$$

In order to understand the exchange rate dynamics implied by this specification, let us work on a simple exercise. Assume that the interest rates in the US go up (i.e. $i \uparrow$) at the end of time t, while the interest rates in the UK (i.e. i^*) do not change. Because this adjustment took place at the end of time t, the closing value of the spot rate, i.e. s_t must have already been revealed – hence, it cannot change. The only adjustment that can take place on the RHS of the UIP equation requires f to go up. Remember that $f = ln(F)$. Since log transformations are monotonic transformations, an increasing f means a higher F, i.e. a higher forward rate. The meaning of all these in plain English is that according to the claim of the UIP, if the interest rates in the US go up, the Pound should appreciate. That finding is very much in line with the no-arbitrage assumption of the UIP: If investments that are made in Dollar terms earn more because of the increasing interest rates in the US, those excess returns should be lost when converting US Dollars to Pounds. However, that finding, on the other hand, is not in conformity with the empirical observations because, usually, the opposite holds in reality: When the interest rates go up in a country (say the US), its currency (i.e. Dollar) appreciates since more investors would be lured by higher returns. Figure 2.1 indicates the trajectories of the daily US Dollar (USD) price of

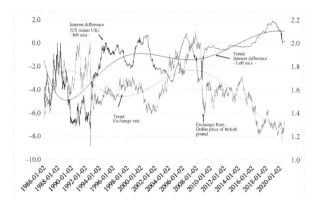

Figure 2.1 USD/GBP exchange rate vs. US/UK interest rate differential

Source: Data is from St. Louis Federal Reserve Economic Data (FRED) Database.

Notes: Interest rates are the three-month LIBOR rates in USD and in GBP.

Trend series show the sextic polynomial approximations.

the British Pound (GBP), along with interest rate differential between the US and the UK from 2 January 1980 to 14 August 2020 as an example.

The trend curves of both series clearly indicate to us that the US Dollar was inclined to appreciate whenever the difference between the US interest rates and the UK interest rates increased in favor of US assets. This is the opposite of the prediction of the UIP.

Notes

1 The rules used here are i) $ln(a/b) = ln(a) - ln(b)$,
    ii) $ln(a \times b) = ln(a) + ln(b)$, and
    iii) $ln(1 + a) \approx a$ *given that a is a sufficiently small number.*
2 Note that s_{t+1} and s_t are the log values of the forward and spot exchange rates. Hence, their difference is equal to the percentage change in the exchange rates.

3 Nonlinearity of the exchange rates

Just because the UIP rule does not hold does not mean that there is no relationship between the interest rates and the exchange rates. Quite the contrary; there might be a stable relationship between them, though this relationship might be opposite of the one that is dictated by the UIP rule. Such an adverse relationship would still provide us with important information for predicting the exchange rates. Such a relationship would indeed be highly useful for fund managers and investors of any kind. However, it would pose a conundrum, as well. It would mean that the exchange rate market, despite being so liquid and so big in transaction volume, is unable to clear away arbitrage opportunities. Long-lasting arbitrage opportunities, in a market like that, sounds weird, but this absurd finding would nevertheless not cripple the usefulness of an adverse relationship for prediction purposes. The worst-case scenario would be to find a statistically insignificant relationship between the two variables in a robust manner using different currency pairs over different time periods.

The relationship between the changes in the exchange rates and the differences in the interest rates has therefore been a puzzle of international finance since the work of Eugene Fama in 1984 when Fama converted the deterministic UIP specification to its stochastic counterpart to test for whether UIP was holding or not. The Fama equation is as follows:

$$\Delta s_{t+1} = \alpha + \beta \left(i - i^* \right)_t + \varepsilon_t \quad \text{(Fama equation)}$$

Uncovered interest parity (UIP), the parity condition relating the interest rate differentials to the nominal exchange rate returns, as previously stated, implies that if investors are risk-neutral and have rational expectations, the future percentage changes in the exchange rates should be determined by the current interest rate differentials between countries (Froot and Thaler, 1990). UIP is usually tested by a simple regression, in which the nominal change in the exchange rate is the dependent variable while the interest rate differential is the independent variable (see the preceding Fama equation). The null hypothesis assumes that the slope coefficient is positive and 1, hence the assertion is that the domestic currency has to depreciate when domestic interest rates exceed foreign interest rates and this has to be a direct relationship. However, empirical evidence almost universally rejects the UIP hypothesis (Chinn and Meredith, 2005). Moreover, most of the datasets tested over the years reported negative slope coefficients. That is to say, on the average, there exists long-lasting profit opportunity from arbitrage in currency carry trade. But as I have said previously, this situation is not a big problem for prediction purposes. It is like having a friend who almost always chooses the wrong team to bet on in soccer games. Since soccer is played in between two teams and since your friend is extremely good at finding the losing team, you could still profit from your friend's misfortune by simply betting on the opposite team of his choice.

Some studies found slope coefficients with the correct signs, though. Examples for this sort of paper are Bansal and Dahlquist (BD, 2000), Chaboud and Wright (CW, 2003), and Chinn and Meredith (CM, 2005). BD reported that the often-found negative correlation is confined to developed economies only and state-dependent, i.e. they report that they observed negative correlations in developed countries data whenever the US interest rate exceeded foreign interest rates. That is to say, BD had to relax the linear specification of the Fama equation in order to find state-dependent UIP-confirmative results.

CW have considered the interest-earning overnight positions and worked with high-frequency data. A foreign exchange account that is not closed before a specific time (17:00 New York time) is considered an open account for the whole night and overnight interest gain accrues on it. Therefore, opening a position right before the specified time is almost a riskless transaction in the foreign exchange market since the value of the foreign exchange rate would, probably, not change dramatically (almost no exchange rate risk) but the interest gain would be guaranteed. The authors reported support for UIP, but it holds only for this limited and special period. Like BD, CW also had to relax the linearity assumption of the Fama equation, as you can tell.

CM studied the opposite end of the same question using the long-horizon data. They found that the coefficients on interest differentials start to be of the correct sign and most of them become closer to the predicted value of positive one as the time horizon gets larger.

Aside from those, many possible theories have been proposed before now in an attempt to explain the puzzle. Although a little old now, Engel (1996) is still an excellent survey of the earliest studies that focused on the risk premia, peso problems, learning issues, irrational expectations and speculative bubbles, and transaction costs as the potential sources of the UIP puzzle.

More recent work has dealt more with the econometric issues such as the unbalanced regressions (Baillie and Kilic, 2006). That is to say, the problems from regressing the nominal changes in the exchange rates which are approximate martingales on the interest differentials which are highly autocorrelated, maybe with a long-memory (Baillie and Bollershev, 1994).

A recent innovation in the econometric modeling of the exchange rates has been the employment of nonlinear techniques such as the threshold autoregressive model and its smooth transition variants such as Smooth Transition and Regression (STR) (Ahmad and Glosser, 2007). I want to save the following chapter for a thorough discussion of the types and causes of nonlinearities in the exchange rates. In the following chapter, I will also speculate a little bit more on the usefulness of models like Threshold Autoregressive Regression and STR.

4 Causes of nonlinearity of the exchange rates

Ahmad and Glosser (2007) argue that due to a widely observed feature of the exchange rates, i.e. the high volatility in the short run and stability in the long run, the exchange rate series should be modeled as nonlinear stationary rather than linear stationary processes. According to Westerhoff (2009), nonlinear exchange rate dynamics may arise due to the nonlinearities inherent in the interactions of the traders in the market. Three possible reasons for the nonlinearity caused by the traders are: i) trading rules may be nonlinear, ii) agents may select between trading strategies, and iii) agents may select between markets. The nonlinear nature of the series is also attributable to the existence of the trading costs and noise trading, as in Panos, Nobay, and Peel (1997) and Killian and Taylor (2003). Although the theoretical proposition for the cause of the nonlinearity of the exchange rates is disputable, the existence of nonlinearity is accepted by the overwhelming majority of the datasets used in the literature.

There exist various tests for detecting nonlinearity in the time series. However, these tests are useful for finding out whether the series is linear or nonlinear. Once nonlinearity is detected, these tests cannot specify any further to select the type of nonlinearity. Specific types should be determined by applying the respective tests for different possible types. Terasvirta's (1994) methodology can be employed to find out whether the nonlinearity happens to be in the form of a smooth transition. GARCH LM tests would help to find the GARCH errors in the series. Furthermore, the theory can impose a specific type of nonlinearity as well. In such a case, the F testing methodology can be used to see whether any type of nonlinearity (unrestricted case) imposed by the theory outperforms the linear option (restricted model).

Nonlinear models in the literature

ARCH and its variants

Pippenger and Goering (1998) refer to Autoregressive Conditional Heteroskedasticity (ARCH) models as the standard nonlinear models in the exchange rate modeling business due to the popularity of those models. However, ARCH methodology is criticized on the grounds that the occurrence of ARCH effects in economic data is not implied by theory in general.

Regime-switches

Another way of capturing nonlinearity in exchange rate data is to use piecewise linear models like the threshold autoregressive (TAR) processes. Unlike ARCH and its variants, threshold processes like TAR are implied by the theory. For example, central banks' policies against market fluctuations such as 'leaning against the wind policy,' where the central banks provide liquidity in response to the selling pressures in the market due to a financial disruption, may cause TAR-type nonlinearities because such policies would require central banks to aim a predetermined threshold level, above which they would be triggered to intervene into the market to provoke mean reversion in exchange rates.

Another complexity that justifies the use of TAR models is the existence of transaction costs. According to that view, traders would not react to exchange rate changes as long as the trading possibilities remain unprofitable due to the transaction costs. Under a scenario like this, the exchange rates would be inclined to move randomly inside a band and return to a mean value outside of it. These sorts of bands, i.e. bands splitting the exchange rate paths into distinct regimes, might be set by a central bank choosing its upper and lower intervention thresholds, as I tried to explain in the preceding paragraph or by the market itself deciding on the borders of profitable and unprofitable trade points.

As for the technical reasons, TAR models are powerful tools capturing the 'nonlinear stationarity' of the exchange rates. Revisiting Ahmad and Glosser's argument, exchange rates series should be modeled as nonlinear stationary rather than linear stationary processes because of a widely observed feature of them: Exchange rate time series typically tend to be notoriously volatile in the short run, while they tend to be stable in the long run. If you wonder how a time series can have these two opposing features at the same time, you should know that exchange rates usually follow random

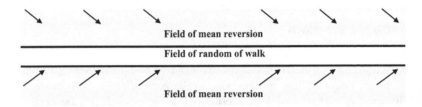

Figure 4.1 The likely regime-dependent movements of exchange rates as meandering series

walk paths – probably inside a certain band. However, they become mean reverting once they move out of the boundaries of the band. Figure 4.1 is a representative figure to help the reader with eyeballing this feature of exchange rates. As you can see in the figure, a band of random walk is sandwiched in between two other bands, where the exchange rate series have mean reversion tendencies (arrows in the figure indicate the direction of the most likely path of the exchange rate series once the exchange rate enters into the fields of mean reversion). This sort of time series, i.e. series which are not stationary in the traditional sense but nonetheless have strong mean reversion tendencies, are known as meandering series. When we say exchange rates are nonlinear stationary, we imply that they are meandering series.

Threshold models have been often used to capture this nonlinear behavior. TAR models assume abrupt switches between the regimes, but in certain cases, it may be more appropriate to assume smooth transitions. Another kind of regime-switching model, known as Smooth Transition Regression (STR) models, allows relatively slower transitions between different regimes. A typical logistic STR (LSTR) model for a dependent variable y_t is defined as follows:

$$y_t = x_t'\beta_0 + x_t'\beta_1 G_{1t} + \varepsilon_t$$

where x_t is the vector of explanatory variables, βs are the parameter vectors, and ε_t is a white noise error. G_{1t} is the transition function and is defined as follows:

$$G_{1t} = G(r_t, \gamma, c) = \left(1 + exp\left\{-\gamma(r_t - c)\right\}\right)^{-1} \tag{4}$$

In this specification, $\gamma > 0$. As γ approaches ∞, the logistic transition function G_{1t} approaches the indicator function and the LSTR model turns into a Switching Regression Model. In the univariate case with an autoregressive term, it becomes a Threshold Autoregressive Regression (TAR) model.

In short, Eq. (4), with its highly flexible specification, indicates to us how close threshold and smooth transition models are to each other from a mathematical point of view. The main difference between them is that the threshold models assume abrupt switches between the regimes, while smooth transition models assume relatively slower transitions from one regime to another, as their name suggests, or you can be either in one regime or the other at any given moment according to the threshold models, while it is possible to exist in an interim state of two regimes at a given moment according to the smooth transition models.

Working with smooth transition models rather than threshold models might seem reasonable to some readers for the reason that if switches between the regimes are abrupt, smooth transition models would capture this anyway with a very high γ estimate, and the estimated path of the G_{1t} function would be highly steep between 0 and 1. However, a threshold model would not be able to show similar flexibility in the opposite case, i.e. if the regime-switches are not abrupt but smooth, because a threshold model, by its very specification, would be inclined to impose abrupt changes even in the case that the true nature of the underlying data indicates smooth transitions. However, as a humble recommendation to those readers, I would like to remind them that they always have to keep in their minds the possibility of overfitting. We are going to revisit the overfitting problem and discuss its true meaning in more detail in the following parts of this book about machine learning algorithms, and we will especially focus on the importance of the bias-variance trade-off for the sake of improved prediction accuracy. However, if I have to shortly summarize the meaning of overfitting in this context, I may say that the traditional statistical and econometric models put too much emphasis on the unbiasedness of their estimates. These models, therefore, try to use every tiny bit of information in the dataset. What if some of the observed data are dirty? What if some of the observed data reflect a one-time anomaly? What if some of the data are only a bunch of outliers and do not carry much information about the regularities of the rest of the population? etc. In such cases, focusing on the out-of-sample prediction accuracy of the model and trying to minimize the estimation variation rather than obsessing over unbiased coefficient estimates might be a better idea.

Chaotic dynamical systems

Other than ARCH and the regime-switching models, another line of nonlinear modeling makes use of the dynamical systems theory. The most widely analyzed process in this area is chaotic motion. Chaotic motion generates data that cannot be easily distinguished from random walk. There exists no known way to identify between random walk and chaos in the time domain. However, in the frequency domain, the two signals can be separated. The major difference between a random walk and chaos is that the random walk cannot be predicted whatsoever, but chaotic processes can be. De Grauwe and Dewachter (1993), using a Dornbusch-type sticky-price monetary model, report that chaotic behavior is likely to exist in the exchange rates. Vandrovych (2006) draws a contrary conclusion. According to Vandrovych, nonlinearity in the exchange rates is captured even by a GARCH structure, but chaos is not the process that explains the nonlinearity in exchange rates. He stresses that chaos can be concluded mistakenly if some necessary technical corrections are not done. In another study, Serletis and Shahmoradi (2004) use Canadian Dollar and US Dollar exchange rates and show that TAR structure is appropriate to use, but there exists no evidence for chaos.

In summary, exchange rates typically follow nonlinear paths. However, our contemporary econometric and statistical knowledge allows us only to identify whether a time series is linear or nonlinear. If nonlinearities are detected, we do not have any statistical test that can tell us the very cause or the causes of this nonlinearity. To make things worse, nonlinear dynamics can come into being as a result of many different reasons. Nonlinear error terms, such as in the case of ARCH or GARCH errors, might be the reason for nonlinearity. Regime-switching behavior of the relationship between the dependent variable and the explanatory variables might be another reason. Chaotic motions in the irregular component of the time series can be yet another reason, etc. Among all these candidates of nonlinear structures, regime-switching models seem to be receiving more attention in the recent literature due to theoretical and technical reasons.

5 Machine learning

Although regime-switching models are highly exciting for their theoretical promise of better capturing the nonlinear dynamics embedded into the exchange rate series, another line of models that are just as exciting are the machine learning models. Machine learning is a branch of data science which simply refers to a group of algorithms that allow a computer to 'learn' from data. Admittedly, 'learning from data' is a vague concept, but you may think of it as figuring out the patterns in the data, highlighting the rules of classification embedded within the data, finding the associations between variables, etc.

Machine learning algorithms are in fact not so distant from the statistical or econometric models in the sense that both the learning algorithms and the statistical or econometric models such as the regime-switching models try to achieve two things: i) explain the data, and ii) predict the future. However, machine learning techniques possess one big advantage over the traditional statistical or econometric models: Machine learning allows for bias-variance trade-off, while unbiasedness remains as an over-emphasized and exaggerated virtue within the domain of traditional statistics and econometrics. In order to have a better understanding of the benefits of using machine learning techniques for exchange rate determination, we might first have to spend some time on this bias-variance trade-off concept.

Bias-variance trade-off

Let us assume that we have made some parametric estimations and we are wondering about the 'goodness' of our statistical estimates. To understand how we can tackle a question like this, further assume that $\beta \in \mathbb{R}$ is the true (but unknown) population parameter value and what we have from our estimation instead of it is a $\hat{\beta}$ value (i.e. an estimate). Since we are interested in finding an answer to how good $\hat{\beta}$ is as an estimated value instead of the true population β, we can specify a measure of loss, i.e. for measuring the loss we are making because of using $\hat{\beta}$ instead of the true population parameter β. Of course, there are a number of ways of characterizing this sort of a measure but a popular choice is the following measure known as the 'squared loss': $E((\hat{\beta} - \beta)^2)$.

With the help of some simple algebra, it is possible to make a useful decomposition of the squared loss as follows. First, add and subtract $E(\hat{\beta})$.

$$E((\hat{\beta} - \beta)^2) = E((\hat{\beta} - E(\hat{\beta}) + E(\hat{\beta}) - \beta)^2)$$

Now we can apply the quadratic formula, i.e. $(a + b)^2 = a^2 + b^2 + 2ab$, to the preceding equation, setting $E(\hat{\beta}) - \beta) = a$ and $\hat{\beta} - E(\hat{\beta}) = b$. Then, we can write the following:

$$E((\hat{\beta} - \beta)^2) = E((E(\hat{\beta}) - \beta)^2) + E((\hat{\beta} - E(\hat{\beta}))^2)$$
$$+ 2E(E(\hat{\beta}) - \beta)(\hat{\beta} - E(\hat{\beta}))$$

Let us recall two of the many rules of the expectation operator. First, $E(E(a)) = E(a)$ if a is a random variable. Second, $E(b) = b$ if b is a scalar. Leaning onto these rules, please see that we can rearrange the last term on the RHS of the preceding equation as follows:

$$2E((E(\hat{\beta}) - \beta)(\hat{\beta} - E(\hat{\beta})) = 2(E(\hat{\beta}) - \beta)(E(\hat{\beta}) - E(\hat{\beta})))$$

Since $E(\hat{\beta}) - E(\hat{\beta}) = 0$, this whole last term on the RHS goes to zero, i.e. $2E((E(\hat{\beta}) - \beta)(\hat{\beta} - E(\hat{\beta}))) = 0$, and we would be left merely with the following notation:

$$E((\hat{\beta} - \beta)^2) = \underbrace{E((E(\hat{\beta}) - \beta)^2)}_{(bias^2)} + \underbrace{E((\hat{\beta} - E(\hat{\beta}))^2)}_{(variance)}$$

In this notation, the first term on the RHS is nothing but the squared value of the $bias(\hat{\beta})$, which quantifies how far the best estimate $\hat{\beta}$ lies from the true β value. The second term is simply the variance of $\hat{\beta}$, which indicates the variance of the sampling distribution. In sum, we just saw that the expected estimation error, measured as the squared loss, is dependent on both the bias and the variance of the estimate.

What we have done so far is: We have shown why the squared loss function is a simple sum of the squared value of the bias and the variance. Now, we need to show why there might be a trade-off between bias and variance and why we have to relax our traditional emphasis on the unbiasedness of the estimates should we want to make better predictions. I want to resort to a visual aid for that purpose.

Assume that we have $y(x)$ and on the following scatter plot we see the x and y observations.

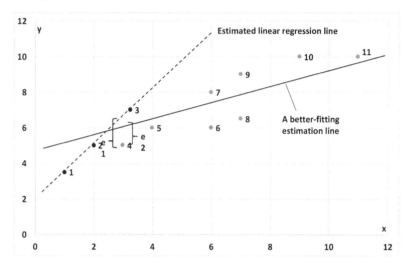

On this scatter plot, as you can see by the labels, there exist 11 points, each showing an ordered pair of (x, y). Let us now assume that we spare the first three points for training purposes and the remaining eight points for testing purposes. If we have to pause here to explain the meaning of training and testing data within the context of machine learning, training datasets are the datasets that we use to parameterize our models, while the testing datasets stay reserved for measuring the prediction accuracy of our estimated models. In this sketchy example, I reserve eight of the data for testing purposes, which means I will only use three of the observations to learn the relationship between x and y. Of course, three data points for learning is extremely insufficient in real life, but please do not forget that what we have here is only a hypothetical example for understanding the very meaning of the bias-variance trade-off.

Turning back to the example, recall that we spared points 1, 2, and 3 for learning. Let us assume that we now employ a traditional linear estimation model in order to learn the x and y relationship, paying only attention to minimizing the estimation bias. That means we would try to achieve the minimum sum of squared residuals from our estimation. In such a case, the estimated regression line would look something as follows.

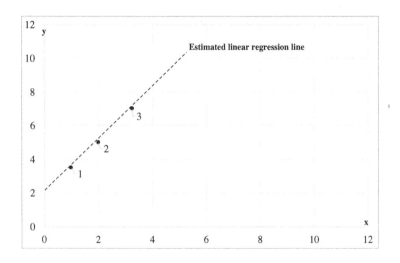

As you might have noticed, the model overfitted onto the three training points without paying any attention to whether these three points have unique characteristics of their own, which cannot be generalizable over the rest of the data points. This overfitting issue resulted from the fact that we only enforced the minimization of the sum of squared residuals. Now, let us put all the test points back to the plot and see what went wrong.

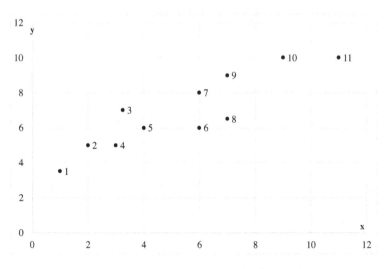

Now we have all the data points back on the plot. The dark points, i.e. points 1, 2, and 3, are the training data, while the gray points are the test data. As you can see once again, the dashed line, i.e. the minimum sum of squared error (SME) regression line, overfits the training data and that is why it makes a terrible job in estimating the rest of the observations (see 'e1,' the error made when estimating point 4). If we had relaxed our unbiasedness criteria and allowed for some variation in the estimations of the data points in the training dataset, we could have drawn another regression line, a better-fitting one, and our out-of-sample prediction accuracy could be much better (see 'e2,' the error made on this line while estimating point 4).

Model validation

With this said, one could duly question how we would know that the solid line should have been picked instead of the dashed one. Plus, why this solid line but not another one with a different slope? The answer to these questions is 'validation.'

In the simplest possible way of definition, validation in statistics is a confirmation activity. It is done to approve (or reject) a model based on the power of its estimations in capturing the true underlying patterns and associations in the dataset. Statistical model validation can either be based on in-sample estimation outputs or out-of-sample estimation outputs. One would pay attention to the in-sample estimation performance of a model if the model is expected to be used for explanatory purposes. A model that is used for explanatory purposes should be able to explain the relations between the explaining variables and the explained variables relatively well given the dataset at hand. The model selection criteria for this type of validation task would naturally focus on the goodness of fit measures and residual diagnostics. One would pay attention to the out-of-sample estimation performance of a model if the model is expected to be used for predictive purposes. Validation of prediction models would rather focus on the prediction accuracy performance of the model when the model is applied to new data. Although validation in statistics is divided into two as validation of explanatory models and validation of prediction models, validation in the field of machine learning means only one thing and it is always the validation of the prediction model.

Now that we have highlighted this slight difference in regard to the meaning of validation in machine learning and traditional statistics, we can move on to describing out-of-sample validation methods in machine learning. The out-of-sample validation techniques that are used in machine learning are usually named cross-validation methods. Cross-validation methods, also known as rotation estimation methods, aim to assess how well the estimations of a model perform when tested on new data. For conducting a cross-validation analysis, the dataset should be first partitioned into two parts as

i) the training dataset, and ii) the testing (or validation) dataset. After the partitioning is done, what comes next is always the same: We first estimate a model on the training dataset and then look whether the results from the training data can be generalizable over the testing data. Although this is roughly the shared logic in the background, cross-validation methods can still be grouped into classes. One way of classifying them is to separate them into two as the i) exhaustive cross-validation and ii) non-exhaustive cross-validation techniques, according to the partitioning of the dataset (Gupta, 2017).[1] Exhaustive cross-validation techniques are those techniques that split the dataset into training and testing parts in all the possible ways. If all the partitioning techniques are not exhausted, the method is simply called a non-exhaustive method.

Non-exhaustive cross-validation methods: hold-out method

The first and simplest non-exhaustive cross-validation method is the hold-out method. In order to understand how hold-out works, assume that we have a dataset of n observations. In the hold-out method, we split this dataset into two parts only once. The real life applications can be done in different ways. For example, we can spare the first k observations for training and the remaining $n - k$ observations automatically become testing dataset. Or we can select k observations randomly from the sample, sparing the unselected observations for testing purposes. There exists no rule in deciding on what n and k should be. However, we can claim as a rule that $k < n$ would be a better choice for the sake of training the model with higher degrees of freedom. It is clear that the hold-out method would be sensitive to outlier effects. Outliers in the training data would cause overfitting, while outliers in the testing data would cause artificially bad prediction results.

Non-exhaustive cross-validation methods: K-fold cross-validation

If an ironclad rule of estimation were ever to be carved in stone, it would most likely read: 'The more is the number of observations, the better it is.' But quite contrary to this rule, we are forced to reserve some of the observations for model testing in the hold-out method. Plus, the hold-out method is sensitive to outliers, as previously stated. To overcome these two issues, researchers generally resort to K-fold cross-validation rather than hold-out method. In the K-fold cross-validation, K stands for a scalar such as 1, 5, 10, etc., n being the maximum possible value for K. Tenfold cross-validation is extremely popular in application, so let us assume we set $K = 10$. What we do is split our dataset into ten subsets. Then we begin to train our model with nine of those (i.e. using 90% of the observations) and test our estimations with the remaining one subset. We repeat this exercise until we use all the subsets at least once for testing purposes. Hence, in the end, we use all the data for testing and for training, leaving no single observations unused. As you can tell, K-fold cross-validation is an iterative but non-exhaustive method, i.e. we iterate our estimations by sliding the training subsets, but we do not consume out all the possibilities of splitting data. Using K-fold cross-validation, we evaluate a model according to the average of the estimation errors from each iteration.

Non-exhaustive cross-validation methods: stratified K-fold cross-validation

Certain types of observations might sometimes be disproportionately represented in datasets. For example, there might be several more observations of negative values in a dataset than positive observations. Similarly, some datasets might contain significantly more men than women or tall people than short people, etc. In such situations, we use stratified K-fold cross-validation, where each subset we form includes observations in the same proportion as the whole sample.

Exhaustive cross-validation methods: leave-p-out and leave-one-out cross-validations

In order to do the leave-p-out cross-validation (LpO CV) on a dataset of n observations, the first step is to choose k observations for training and sparing the remaining $n - k$ observations for testing, just like we do for the non-exhaustive methods. The difference is we have to try all the possible combinations of the split. For example, if $n = 1,000$ and $k = 800$, then the number of times we have to estimate the model with a different split becomes equal to $C_{200}^{1000} = 6.6 \times 10^{215}$, which is clearly a computationally cumbersome number for simulating. That is the main reason why we use K-fold cross-validation, an approximation of LpO CV, rather than LpO CV itself. Another way to overcome this problem is to set $k = n - 1$. When we set $k = n - 1$, we leave only one observation for testing. All the possible ways of splitting the dataset then automatically boil down to a possibly more manageable number of n.

Model types: supervised models vs. unsupervised models

We have so far discussed the important topics in machine learning such as its emphasis on bias-variance trade-off and the various approaches to model validation. We can now progress with a more specific discussion of how we can apply machine learning techniques for predicting the foreign exchange rates. But before focusing on the exchange rates, there is one last machine learning issue that needs to be highlighted. That is the distinction between the supervised and unsupervised models.

For the sake of an easier clarification of the difference between the supervised and unsupervised models, let us assume we a set of m different variables such as $x_1, x_2, x_3, \ldots, x_m$. If we do not impose any type of relationship among these variables and let the machine learning algorithm at hand reveal the hidden associations and correlations between them, figuring out the hidden classes and patterns, etc., then what we do is called unsupervised machine learning.

Supervised machine learning, on the other hand, assumes the dependence of one of the variables to the rest of the variables a priori. That is to say, if we assume for example that x_1 $(x_2, x_3, \ldots, x_m)$, then what we do is called supervised machine learning. Since we have already proven theoretically that the exchange rates should depend on macroeconomic variables such as the interest rates, growth rates, money supplies, etc., supervised techniques seem more appropriate for us.

In the following subsection, I will introduce three different supervised regression techniques that could be extremely helpful in modeling exchange rates since these models pay attention to the trade-off between bias and variance. Bias-variance trade-off is a significantly important point that should never be overlooked in exchange rate predictions due to a well-known phenomenon that is known as the exchange rate disconnect problem. The exchange rate disconnect problem refers to the pervasive empirical observations (especially in developed countries' currencies) that the foreign exchange rates seem usually disconnected from the main economic indicators. The reason for this observed disconnection might be volatility differences between the exchange rate series and the economic variables. Economic variables, compared to the exchange rates, seem highly less volatile. That is a technical issue that economists should take into consideration when modeling the exchange rates using macroeconomic variables. Therefore, models allowing for more estimation variance in the training dataset, for the sake of better prediction accuracy overall, might be useful tools in predicting the foreign exchange rates. In the following subsection, I will introduce three such models: Lasso, Ridge, and Elastic Net regression models, which I will use to predict a real dataset of exchange rates in the next chapter.

Lasso, Ridge, and Elastic Net regressions

All of these three models use regularization techniques in order to avoid overfitting to the training data by penalizing the high-valued coefficient estimates. In other words, they all reduce parameters and simplify (shrink) the model. The whole idea behind penalizing the high-valued coefficients in particular is because these coefficients pose the greatest risk for the out-of-sample performance of the model. The model selection with the correct magnitude of penalty is done by trial and error: We try different penalties first and then sort models from the one with the least overfit to the one with the largest overfit. The least overfitting model is assumed to be the best model with the correct magnitude of the penalty.

The second virtue of regularization is that regularization might help us to deal with multicollinearity issues in the dataset since regularization reduces the models to their more parsimonious forms by eliminating or shrinking the redundant variables such as the linearly dependent ones, which cause multicollinearity.

When we look at the technical part of how regularization works, there we see that it creates biases in the data toward some of the particular values such as the small values near zero. The bias is created through the addition of a penalty to the loss function of the model. If we choose to add to the loss function the absolute values of coefficients as a penalty, this is known as L^1 regularization. A penalty equal to the squared values of the coefficients is called L^2 regularization. Lasso regressions use L^1 regularization penalty, while Ridge regressions use L^2 regularization penalty. A combination of L^1 and L^2 penalties could also be used for regularization purposes, and this is exactly what Elastic Net regressions do.

Note

1 "Cross-Validation in Machine Learning" by Prashant Gupta is an easy and useful article for all levels of students of machine learning. This article can be accessed at: https://towardsdatascience.com/cross-validation-in-machine-learning-72924a69872f

6 Comparing the predictive powers of models

In Chapter 2, we reviewed a number of structural models, namely the uncovered interest parity (UIP) rule, the purchasing power parity rule, the monetary model, the asset-pricing model of exchange rates, a modified Hooper-Morton model, etc. As you will remember, in all these models, the backbone was the relationship between the interest rates and the exchange rates. In fact, all the models were dependent on the UIP rule for relating the macroeconomic variables to exchange rates. That is why I will focus on the UIP rule in this chapter when testing the out-of-sample prediction accuracies of various models.

The models that I will put to test in this chapter can be placed into two groups: i) purely time-series models and ii) structural models. The two purely time series models that I will test are i) a threshold autoregressive regime-switching model (i.e. Threshold Autoregressive Regression, or TAR), and ii) its slow adjusting variant (i.e. a Smooth Transition Regression model, or STR).

As for the structural models, I have already mentioned that I will focus on the relationship between the interest rates and the exchange rates. That is why, in the structural models, the structural variable that I will use is the interest rate differentials between the countries in accordance with the UIP rule. The first structural model that I will test is the Fama equation, which was introduced in Chapter 3, and is nothing but the stochastic counterpart of the deterministic UIP equation. The Fama equation is important for it has been the linear workhorse model of exchange rate determination research since the early 1980s. The second and third structural models that I will test are the regime-switching counterparts of the UIP. One of them is going to be specified as a structural TAR, where the regime-switches would be abrupt, while the second regime-switching model is going to be a structural STR with slow adjustments between the regimes.

The fourth, fifth, and sixth structural models that I will use are the Lasso, Ridge, and Elastic Net models. Finally, all these models are going to be compared against each other and also against a random walk model with respect to their out-of-sample prediction accuracies.

Table 6.1 indicates all of the models that will be tested in this chapter together in a neat way. In the table, the type of each model is categorized

Table 6.1 Various candidate models for predicting the foreign exchange rates

Type	Name	Specification and parameterization rule (Rule)	
T	TAR	**Specification:**	$\Delta s_{t+1} = \begin{cases} \alpha_1 + \beta_{11}(\Delta s_t) + \dots + \beta_{1p}(\Delta s_{t-p+1}) \, if \; r < \theta \\ \alpha_2 + \beta_{21}(\Delta s_t) + \dots + \beta_{2q}(\Delta s_{t-q+1}) \, if \; r \geq \theta \end{cases}$
			where r is a transition variable and θ is the threshold
		Rule:	min SSR
T	STR	**Specification:**	$\left[\alpha_1 + \beta_{11}(\Delta s_t) + \dots + \beta_{1p}(\Delta s_{t-p+1}) \right]$
			$+ G_{1t}\left[\alpha_1 + \beta_{11}(\Delta s_t) + \dots + \beta_{1p}(\Delta s_{t-p+1}) \right] + \varepsilon_t$
			where G_{1t} is the transition function
		Rule:	min SSR
S-L	Fama equation	**Specification:**	$\alpha + \beta(i - i^*)_t + \varepsilon_t$
		Rule:	min SSR
S-RS	Structural TAR	**Specification:**	$\Delta s_{t+1} = \begin{cases} \alpha_1 + \beta_1(i - i^*)_t + \varepsilon_{1t} \, if \; r < \theta \\ \alpha_2 + \beta_2(i - i^*)_t + \varepsilon_{2t} \, if \; r \geq \theta \end{cases}$
			where r is a transition variable and θ is the threshold
		Rule:	min SSR

(Continued)

Table 6.1 (Continued)

Type	Name	Specification and parameterization rule (Rule)	
S-RS	Structural STR	**Specification:**	$[\alpha_1 + \beta_1(i-i^*)_t] + G_{tt}[\alpha_2 + \beta_2(i-i^*)_t]_t + \varepsilon_t$
		Rule:	min SSR
S-ML	Lasso regression	**Specification:**	$\alpha + \beta(i-i^*)_t + \varepsilon_t$
		Rule:	min $(SSR + \lambda(|\hat{\alpha}| + |\hat{\beta}|)$
S-ML	Ridge regression	**Specification:**	$\alpha + \beta(i-i^*)_t + \varepsilon_t$
		Rule:	min $(SSR + \lambda(\hat{\alpha}^2 + \hat{\beta}^2)$
S-ML	Elastic Net regression	**Specification:**	$\alpha + \beta(i-i^*)_t + \varepsilon_t$
		Rule:	min $(SSR + \lambda[(1-\theta)(\hat{\alpha}^2 + \hat{\beta}^2) + \theta(|\hat{\alpha}| + |\hat{\beta}|)]$
T	Random walk	**Specification:**	$\Delta s_{t+1} = \Delta s_t + \varepsilon_t$
		Rule:	model is enforced to have unit root

with capital 'T,' 'S-L,' 'S-RS,' and 'S-ML' letters, which respectively stand to indicate that these models are 'time series,' 'linear structural,' 'structural regime-switching,' or 'structural machine learning' models. The exact specification of each model is presented in the third column. The parameterization for each model is given in the third column as well. For example, let us look at the first row. There we see the specification of the purely time series TAR model and read that the estimated parameter values are the ones that makes the sum of the squared residuals the lowest. The lowest sum of squared residuals, by the way, is the total of the sum of squared residuals of the first regime and the sum of squared residuals of the second regime.

In the following part of this chapter, I will estimate all these models in the table one by one and compare their out-of-sample prediction accuracies on the basis of the mean squared prediction errors (MSPE) and mean absolute errors (MAE) they produce.

The exchange rate observations that I will use in order to estimate these models are the USD/JPY and USD/AUD exchange rates. USD/JPY exchange rate indicates the Japanese Yen worth of 1 US Dollar, and similarly, USD/AUD exchange rate indicates the Australian Dollar worth of 1 US Dollar. The reason that I chose these two currencies is because the US Dollar is the unrivaled single currency vehicle in the international financial system, and that is why it is also the most widely traded currency in the world by far. The Japanese Yen also is also an important currency in the international financial system since it is persistently among the most widely traded currencies. Plus, it is an important currency in international trade since Japan is one of the major export powerhouses of the world. Additionally, the Japanese Yen is also a popular funding currency in international currency carry trades. Finally, the Japanese Yen has been allowed to float since 1973, and that is why it is one of the currencies with the longest history of free float. As for the reason why I chose USD/AUD exchange rate, AUD is yet another popular international currency, just like the USD and JPY, but its popularity depends on highly different factors: AUD is one of the leading investment currencies in the international currency carry trade business, for the interest rates in Australia tend to be higher than virtually any other developed country, with the possible exception of New Zealand.

The dataset includes monthly observations from May 1979 through May 2020. Exchange rate data was retrieved from the FED's webpage, while the interest rates data was retrieved from the Federal Reserve Economic Data (FRED) database of the St. Louis Fed. The interest rates for the US and Japan are the three-month (or 90-day) yields of Certificates of Deposit for the US and Japan. For the US and Australia, three-month (or 90-day) interbank rates are used. The difference between the US and the Japan interest rates, along with the difference between the US and the Australian interest rates, are sketched in Figure 6.1. The US interest rates were generally

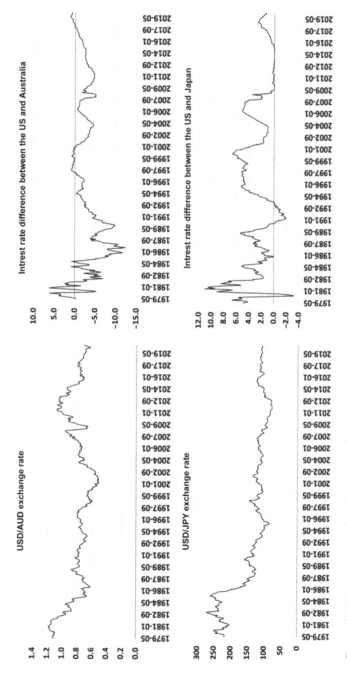

Figure 6.1 Interest rates and exchange rates for USD/JPY and USD/AUD

higher than the Japanese interest rates for the entire 41 years covered, with the exception of only a handful of years, while the Australian interest rates were generally higher than the US interest rates, again with a few years of exceptions.

The Fama equation

I will first estimate the Fama equation, i.e. the linear stochastic counterpart of the UIP model, since it has appeared in myriad empirical papers over the decades as the workhorse linear model of the relationship between interest rates and exchange rates. The exact specifications of this model are already presented in Table 6.1. Therefore, I am not going to repeat it.

I rather want to give information about the computer packages and software that I have used in estimating the models in Table 6.1. I used R and Eviews for estimating the Fama equation. I also used R for estimating the Lasso, Ridge, and Elastic Net regressions. I used Eviews for the smooth transition models. I used Eviews for TAR models, as well. Eviews is a highly capable software with a very user-friendly graphical user interface, while R is a full-fledged vector-based programming language, which requires at least some basic programming skills. R is widely used among statisticians and data analysts for its superior data analysis capabilities, which continue to expand with the introduction of new packages. R is free, while only a lite (yet highly capable) version of Eviews can be used by scholars and students for free.

I have already said that I have used R for estimating the Fama equation. I provide my R code to the readers of this book shortly. To be clear, following is the R code of the Fama equation model and that code is written for estimating the USD/JPY data as an example. The same code could, of course, be used easily for estimating the USD/AUD data, as well, with minor modifications of the variables' names. Let us focus on explaining some of the command lines in the following code now. First of all, you should have R installed on your computer. Assume that you have installed R and opened it. After opening R, you must change the working directory. For example, if you have a 'csv' file named 'BookDataset' on your desktop, which contains the data you will use in your analysis, you should change the working directory as desktop and then upload your data file. Note that your dataset could, of course, be stored somewhere else on your computer. All you have to do in a case like that is to change your working directory accordingly and then upload your file. The following code first uploads that dataset to R and then does the linear estimation of the Fama equation where the percentage change in the USD/JPY exchange rate over three months is the dependent variable and the difference between the three-month interest rates in the US and Japan is the independent variable.

Last but not least, the pound sign (#) indicates the simple texts, i.e. lines starting with a pound sign are text lines and would not be run by the program. That is why all the lines starting with # in what follows are simply there for communication purposes. Using them, I have tried to explain to the reader the meaning of the lines in the code.

```
################################################################
# R CODES FOR ESTIMATING THE FAMA EQUATION AND CALCULATING    #
# THE MSPE AND MAE OF ITS PREDICTIONS                         #
################################################################
# with the following 'read.csv' command, we upload a dataset
from our computer to R

data = read.csv("RoutledgeBookData.csv")
n = nrow(data) # number of rows in the dataset is fed into an
object named 'n'

# data partitioning: we can partition data into training and
# testing sets in multiple ways below are the codes for random
# sampling of the dataset as 90% of the data spared for training
# purposes and remaining 10% spared for testing. Before using
# the codes, do not forget to erase the '#' sign in front of
# the command lines.

# ind = sample(2, nrow(data), replace = TRUE, prob = c(0.90,0.10))
# data_train = data[ind==1,]
# data_test = data[ind==2,]

# or we can apply the simple Hold-out method for partitioning.
# Below are the codes retaining the first 90% of the observations
# for training and using the rest for testing

data_train = data[1:as.integer(0.90*nrow(data)),]
data_test = data[(as.integer(0.90*nrow(data))+1):nrow(data),]

# remember that we are estimating the fama equation for USD/JPY
# as an example the columns of our dataset are as follows (in
# order):
# 'X' 'X3mchgUSDAUD' 'X3mchgUSDJPY' 'US_JPYintdiff'
# 'US_AUDintdiff' 'stdevusdaud' 'stdevusdjpy'
# therefore we only need the 3rd column X3mchgUSDJPY,
# i.e. 3 monthly change in the USD/JPY exchange rate, and the 4th
# column US_JPYintdiff, i.e. the interest rate differential
# between the US and Japan

training_interest_differential = data_train[ ,4]
training_exchange_rate = data_train[ ,3]
```

```
testing_interest_differential = data_test[ ,4]
testing_exchange_rate = data_test[ ,3]

# train the model using the training dataset
    model.lm = lm(training_exchange_rate~training_interest_
    differential, data = data_train)

# make the out-of-sample prediction of the model using the
    testing data
    pred = model.lm$coefficients[1]+model.lm$coefficients[2]*
    data_test[,3]

y = as.matrix(testing_exchange_rate)
yhat = as.matrix(pred)
errors = yhat-y
errorssquared = errors*errors
errorsabsolute = abs(errors)

# calculation of the Mean Squared Prediction Error and Mean
    Absolute Error of the model
    MSPE_fama = mean(errorssquared)
    MAE_fama = mean(errorabsolute)
##############################-0-##############################
```

The dataset I have used in this book, titled RoutledgeBookData, will be made available on request, both as a 'csv' and 'xlsx' file, to any researcher who might feel interested in investigating the data. Plus, some of the readers might want to replicate the analyses as an amusing teaching exercise. They can easily do the replications using the code on those pages and the data stored in the repository. Having noted that, I want to reveal the results in Table 6.2.

Purely time series TAR and STR models

In order to estimate the purely time series TAR and STR models, let us open in Eviews the RoutledgeBookData.xlsx file, i.e. the Excel version of the same dataset that I used in estimating the MSPE and MAE values from the Fama equation.

Table 6.2 MSPE and MAE values for the estimation errors of the Fama equation

	USD/JPY	*USD/AUD*
MSPE	6.294303	13.14589
MAE	1.932033	2.855215

After uploading the observations to Eviews, click on the 'Quick' menu at the top. A drop-down menu that looks like the one here will open:

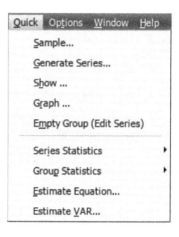

Navigate to select the 'Estimate Equation . . .' option. In the box that opens, change the method to 'THRESHOLD' under the estimation settings.

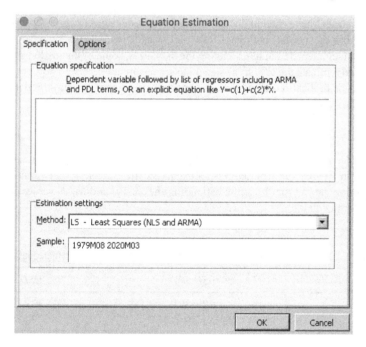

Now you should be facing a screen as follows:

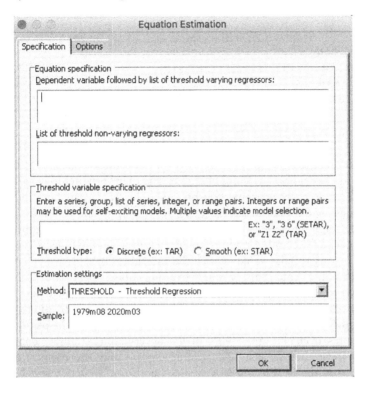

As you see, Eviews gives its users the option to select TAR or a smooth version of it, named STAR, which is no different than our STR model. Look carefully and notice that the period of the sample is reported in the box at the bottom. Eviews allows the manipulation of this sample period. Now, for our example, let us shorten the sample from 1979m08 to 2016m02. This means that we are restricting the observations only to a period stretching from August 1979 to February 2016, i.e. we are taking 90% of the whole dataset. Remember that we have employed 90% of the observations using the hold-out method in the previous section while estimating the Fama equation. We are creating the same training dataset for our TAR and STR models. Now we can estimate these two models one by one. In the Options tab, the tab that you can see at the top of the dialog box in the first screenshot, we set the trimming option to 15%, i.e. we discard the outliers and do the estimation in a self-exciting way. Self-excitement within the regime-switching models jargon refers

Table 6.3 MSPE and MAE values for the estimation errors of the TAR and STR time series models

	USD/JPY	*USD/AUD*
MSPE_TAR	6.290992	13.98764
MAE_TAR	1.789345	2.615223
MSPE_STR	6.371232	13.341267
MAE_STR	2.191891	3.0321234

to the situation that past value(s) of the dependent variable is (are) used as the regime-switching variable. The regime-switching variable, by the way, is the variable that provokes the transitions between the regimes. In a model of two regimes, for example, one of the regimes would reign when the transition variable takes values below a threshold level and the other regime would kick in when the transition variable begins to take values above the threshold level. If we return to our example, since this is a self-exciting model, past values of the exchange rate changes are assumed to provoke regime-switches. Values from 1–6 are tried in the 'threshold variable specification' box. With those settings, I have done the estimation and used the parameter estimates from the initial 90% of the observations (training data) in order to predict the last 10% (testing data). Using the errors, I have calculated the MSPE and MAE values both for USD/JPY and USD/AUD exchange rates (Table 6.3).

Structural TAR and STR models

The structural TAR and STR models that I have employed in this book resemble their purely time series counterparts with two major differences. First, they rely on a structural variable, and that structural variable is the interest rate differential between the countries. Second, regimes are provoked not in a self-exciting manner but by an external transition variable. The transition variable that I have used for the structural models is the standard deviation of the exchange rates.

If I have to explain the reason why I have chosen the standard deviation of the exchange rates as the transition variable, I cannot think of a paragraph explaining my reason better than the following one that I have taken from the 78th annual report of the Bank for International Settlements (BIS). To be more precise, on 30 June 2008, BIS announced its 78th Annual Report for the financial year that began on 1 April 2007 and ended on 31 March 2008. In

Table 6.4 MSPE and MAE values for the estimation errors of the structural TAR and STR models

	USD/JPY	USD/AUD
MSPE_TAR	5.903264	11.674726
MAE_TAR	1.648353	1.995278
MSPE_STR	5.637235	12.182258
MAE_STR	1.684697	2.932346

the relevant chapter of the report regarding the foreign exchange markets, the following lines were noteworthy.*

> Foreign exchange markets experienced a substantial increase in volatility in August 2007. This marked an important change in the factors driving market developments. Prior to August, historically low volatility and large interest rate differentials had underpinned cross-border capital flows that put downward pressure on funding currencies . . . , and supported high-yielding currencies. [As a result of the heightened volatility] there was a substantial reassessment of expected monetary policy actions as the dimensions of the problems in financial markets became more apparent. In this environment, factors such as expected growth differentials, which have an important bearing on the future path of monetary policy, became more of a focal point for market sentiment than the prevailing level of interest rates.

As you must have noticed, there was an implicit assumption at the back of the mind of the analyst as these lines were written: The timing of the transitions from one regime to another is determined by the level of volatility. Upon reading these lines, I have decided to use the standard deviations of the exchange rates as a gauge of volatility in the foreign exchange rate markets. As was done in the previous section, I again used Eviews for estimating the structural TAR and STR models. The MSPE and MAE values that I have calculated are shown in Table 6.4.

Lasso, Ridge, and Elastic Net regressions

Using USD/JPY and USD/AUD exchange rates, we have already estimated the out-of-sample MSPE and MAE values of five different models. Four of

---

* This excerpt appeared at the beginning of the 5th chapter about the foreign exchange rates beginning on the 75th page of the 78th Annual Report of the BIS. Following URL provides the World Wide Web link to these lines. https://www.bis.org/publ/arpdf/ar2008e5.pdf

these models are nonlinear. The only linear model that we have estimated so far is the Fama equation model. That small ratio of linear to nonlinear models almost mirrors the contemporary situation in the empirical exchange rate literature. An increasing number of studies are embracing nonlinear models over their linear counterparts for a good reason: Exchange rate series typically follow nonlinear paths.

We have already discussed in some detail the potential reasons for non-linearities that could be observed in exchange rates. Remember that nonlinearities could happen as a result of many potential reasons. If we need to recall them, ARCH or GARCH effects in errors could cause nonlinearities. Nonlinearities could be observed as a result of regime-switches, as well. Brownian motion of the irregular component of the time series could also make exchange rates nonlinear, etc.

The question that I want to pose in this section is whether we discarded the linear models too early. Could linear models that make a trade-off between bias and variance be used for predicting the exchange rates at least for longer prediction horizons (since in the longer prediction horizons, ARCH/ GARCH effects are known to lose their strength and the exchange rates are known to follow a mean reverting path)?

Here, I want to share an R code for estimating the MSPE and MAE of three such linear models, i.e. the Lasso, Ridge, and Elastic Net models, and run this code on the dataset of monthly observations of the USD/JPY and USD/AUD exchange rates.

In order to run the following code, the 'glmnet' package in R should be installed. If you do not have this package, you can install it with the following lines:

```
# install.packages("glmnet")
# Now we can call the glmnet library and load our dataset
```

One final issue that needs clarification before I share the code is the meaning of the alpha parameter that you will see in the following code. Remember the penalty of the Elastic Net regression that I shared in Table 6.1. As a rule, Elastic Net regression tries to minimize the following loss function, where the second term is the penalty:

$$\min\left(SSR + \underbrace{\lambda[(1-\theta)\left(\hat{\alpha}^2 + \hat{\beta}^2\right) + \theta\left(|\hat{\alpha}| + |\hat{\beta}|\right)}_{\text{Penalty in Elastic Net regression}}\right)$$

Now, let us also recall the penalties of the Ridge and Lasso regressions. Ridge penalty is $\lambda\left(\hat{\alpha}^2 + \hat{\beta}^2\right)$, while Lasso penalty is $\lambda\left(|\hat{\alpha}| + |\hat{\beta}|\right)$. The θ parameter as you must have noticed is a tuning parameter. If θ is equal to zero, Elastic Net penalty boils down to Ridge penalty. If θ is equal to 1, it boils down to Lasso penalty. In the glmnet package in R, θ parameter, i.e. the tuning parameter, is called alpha. While reading the following code, please keep that mind.

```
###############################################################
# R CODES FOR ESTIMATING THE LASSO, RIDGE AND ELASTIC NET    #
# EQUATIONS AND CALCULATING THEIR MSPE AND MAE VALUES        #
###############################################################
library(glmnet)
data = read.csv("RoutledgeBookData.csv)

n = nrow(data) # Number of observations

x = data[,4]
y = data[,3]

# partitioning of the data into training and testing parts
# 90% of the data will be spared for training, 10% for testing

train_rows = sample(1:n,  .90*n)
x.train = x[train_rows, ]
x.test = x[-train_rows, ]

y.train = y[train_rows]
y.test = y[-train_rows]

######################################
# CASE 1:
# alpha = 0, Ridge regression
#
######################################

alpha0.fit = glmnet(x.train, y.train, alpha = 0, family = "gaussian")

######################################
# note that we could use cv.glmnet function as well for training
# the data, which optimizes the model using 10-fold cross-
# validation. Then the code would look like as follows:
# cv.glmnet(x.train, y.train, type.measure="mse", alpha=0,
#   family="gaussian")
######################################

# Run the Ridge model on the testing dataset

alpha0.predicted = predict(alpha0.fit,  s=alpha0.fit$lambda.min,
newx=x.test)

# Mean Squared Prediction Error (MSPE) and Mean Absolute Error
  (MAE) of the Ridge model
```

```
errors = (y.test - alpha0.predicted)
MSPE_Ridge = mean(errors^2)
MAE_Ridge = abs(errors)

###############################
## CASE 2:
## alpha = 1, Lasso Regression
##
###############################

alpha1.fit = glmnet(x.train, y.train, alpha=1, family="gaussian")

alpha1.predicted = predict(alpha1.fit, s=alpha1.fit$lambda.min,
newx=x.test)

# Mean Squared Prediction Error (MSPE) and Mean Absolute Error
 (MAE) of the Lasso model

errors = (y.test - alpha1.predicted)
MSPE_Lasso = mean(errors^2)
MAE_Lasso = abs(errors)

# we can see the results for MSPE or MAE, simply by calling
 these objects

###############################
## CASE 3:
## alpha values changing from 0 to 1 with steps of size = 0.01
## A Numerical Approach to Elastic Net Modelling
###############################

# Let us try alpha values from 0 to 1 by changing alpha = i/100

list.of.fits = list()
for (i in 0:100) {

  fit.name = paste0("alpha", i/100)

  list.of.fits[[fit.name]] =
   cv.glmnet(x.train, y.train, type.measure="mse", alpha=i/100,
    family="gaussian")

# In the above line, I am using cv.glmnet function instead of
 glmnet function.
# their difference is cv.glmnet automatically does 10-fold
 cross-validation

}

# predict the values in the testing dataset
```

```
results = data.frame()
for (i in 0:10) {
  fit.name = paste0("alpha", i/10)

# use each model to predict 'y' given the testing dataset

predicted =
  predict(list.of.fits[[fit.name]],
    s = list.of.fits[[fit.name]]$lambda.1se, newx=x.test)

# calculate the Mean Squared Prediction Error (MSPE) and Mean
  Absolute Error (MAE)

errors = (y.test - predicted)

MSPE = mean((errors)^2)
MAE = mean(abs(error))

# store the results

  temp = data.frame(alpha=i/10, mse=MSPE, fit.name=fit.name)
  results = rbind(results, temp)
}

# we can view the results for MSPE by calling the results object
  as follows
# if we change the mse value above and set it equal to MAE, we
  get the results for MAE

results
######################## - 0 - ############################
```

Now we have estimated the MSPE and MAEs of all the models except the random walk. In order to estimate the MSPE and MAE of the random walk model, all we have to do is to get the sliding differences between the observations. Assume that you have the observation for February 2020 in your testing dataset. The estimated value of this observation according to the random walk model would be the observation in January 2020. Table 6.5 presents the MSPE and MAE estimations from each model for USD/JPY and USD/AUD. As you can see, the random walk model is the superior forecaster in most cases.

As Table 6.2 shows, the random walk model is a very strong predictor of the exchange rates. This is already a long-standing and empirically proven fact, and there is nothing surprising with it. The true blow that this table deals us is that it shows how powerless the alternative models are before a simple driftless random walk model. Even after re-specifying the traditional models in order to adapt them to the observed nonlinearities in

Table 6.5 MSPE and MAE values comparison of the prediction models

		USD/JPY	*USD/AUD*
Fama equation	MSPE	6.294303	13.14589
Random walk	MSPE	5.610298	11.549823
TAR (time series)	MSPE	6.290992	13.98764
TAR (structural)	MSPE	5.903264	11.674726
STR (time series)	MSPE	6.371232	13.341267
STR (structural)	MSPE	5.637235	12.182258
Lasso	MSPE	10.342563	14.090246
Ridge	MSPE	7.126322	9.662522
Elastic Net	MSPE	5.557535	7.394562
Fama equation	MAE	1.932033	2.855215
Random walk	MAE	1.629913	2.012245
TAR (time series)	MAE	1.789345	2.615223
TAR (structural)	MAE	1.648353	1.995278
STR (time series)	MAE	2.191891	3.032123
STR (structural)	MAE	1.684697	2.932346
Lasso	MAE	3.722195	4.009146
Ridge	MAE	2.363528	3.840313
Elastic Net	MAE	1.933211	2.469941

the exchange rates or using machine learning techniques benefiting from the bias-variance trade-off approach, we could not make them produce better prediction results than the random walk, although some of the regime-switching specifications performed quite close to the random walk (and even slightly surpassed the random walk model in two cases without being able to systematically beat it).

That is why I want us all to take a step back and ponder what we really want when we attempt to predict the exchange rates. My question is that we try to predict the future exchange rates, but why do we want to predict the exchange rates in the first place? Generally, we only need to know where (in what direction) the exchange rates will move in the future rather than the exact value they will assume in the future. That is to say, for policy-makers, for investors, for business people, etc., knowing whether the US Dollar will likely appreciate in the future or depreciate is more than enough information most of the time. Of course, there are times when we need a point estimation, too (for example, knowing only the direction of the future exchange rates would not be enough for an investment planner trying to forecast the probability of a planned investment project; or a banker trying to sell or buy currency options would be interested in a point estimate of the exchange rates). However, in most cases, a reliable estimation of the direction of the change would be enough for making profits or preventing losses. Therefore, I want to change our prediction strategy in the following chapter and see if it is possible to estimate the direction of the future exchange rates even though we cannot make satisfactory point estimations. My benchmark in the next chapter will be the random walk model for the obvious reason.

7 Should we focus on sign estimations rather than point estimations?

As I tried to explain in the final paragraph of the previous chapter, it is highly unlikely that we would derive significantly more benefit if we could make good point estimations of the exchange rates rather than making good direction (sign) estimations. Let me explain this using an example of a hypothetical XYZ currency. Assume that 1 USD buys 2.300 XYZ today. For the investors and business people, policymakers, etc., it would not make a difference whether 1 USD would buy 2.345 XYZ in the future or 2.356. What matters in most cases is to know whether it would buy more than 2.300 XYZ or less than 2.300 XYZ.

Remember that the random walk model has repeatedly proven its superiority as a forecasting tool against any other time series or structural model in the last 40 years. Then, let us focus on what the random walk is doing. The random walk is telling us that the best prediction of the future exchange rates is the last observed value of the exchange rate. However, due to its white noise disturbance, which is symmetrically centered around zero, it is also telling us that there exists a 50% chance that the future exchange rate might be higher than the last observed value, while there exists another 50% chance that it might be lower. The accuracy of that prediction is 100%, as you can tell. If you think that way, in fact, the random walk model is not doing much. But it is doing what it does with superb accuracy. Therefore, if we can develop a prediction model which tells us something slightly different, such as "there exists a 51% chance that the future exchange rate will be higher and 49% chance that it will be lower," and furthermore, does that with very high accuracy, then even such a loose model could become superior to the random walk. In order to develop an estimation model like that, I want to introduce the Classification and Regression Tree analysis, more popularly known as the CART analysis. After this introduction, I will attempt to develop a random forest model of exchange rates based on the monetary model.

CART analysis

I have taken the following lines from the webpage of the US Environmental Protection Agency. A simple method like CART analysis could not be explained more confusingly than this.

> Classification and regression tree (CART) analysis recursively partitions observations in a matched data set, consisting of a categorical (for classification trees) or continuous (for regression trees) dependent (response) variable and one or more independent (explanatory) variables, into progressively smaller groups.

Instead of making a hard-to-understand definition, I will try to explain CART analysis in an easier way using an example. Assume for the sake of this example that we have a clothing store and we are selling t-shirts there. Say we have been in this business for more than 30 years, a hint of our tremendous experience. After all those years, we should be able to claim quite confidently that the preferences of customers differ strikingly based on a number of factors such as their gender, age, etc. Let us therefore finally assume that those years in the business have gifted us a mental map showing different t-shirt styles (i.e. polo, baseball, basic, v-neck) and the most probable customer profiles matching them (Figure 7.1).

This mental map, by itself, is nothing but a classification tool. It shows us how we have classified over the years our customers' most likely t-shirt preferences in our mind and provides us with clues on what our offerings should be to our future customers in order to facilitate sales. For example, it could be a good idea to recommend baseball t-shirts should the customer be a young male, while basic t-shirts might be more alluring for older female

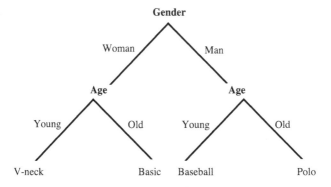

Figure 7.1 An exemplary representation of a hypothetical decision tree

customers. We can make predictions like if a customer is male and older, the t-shirt he will purchase is most likely going to be a polo. In short, our experience has shaped this decision tree and we can use it for making predictions. The explained (or predicted) variable is the t-shirt style, while age and gender are the explaining (or predicting) variables. That is why this mental map seems to be the outcome of a supervised learning process (i.e. for many years, we have observed the various factors that have associations with the style of the t-shirts sold and we have concluded that two of them, namely the age and gender of the customer, have useful information – in short, we have a dependent variable, i.e. t-shirt styles, and a set of independent variables affecting it. Remember that such models with a dependent variable are called supervised learning models). If we think this way, the preceding sketch is nothing but a decision tree, an outcome of a supervised learning process, and our efforts of many years to understand the relationship between the t-shirt styles and age and gender is CART analysis in its most instinctive form.

In this example, we have attempted to explain the factors that are affecting the t-shirt preferences of customers. The t-shirt styles are non-numeric observations. That is why the sum of all the reflexive and cognitive efforts we must have unconsciously conducted at the back of our mind while drawing our mental map would be called a classification analysis in data science jargon. If we tried to explain a numeric variable, it would be categorized as regression analysis. In sum, there exist two different kinds of analyses that can be done to produce a decision tree: i) classification analysis and ii) regression analysis. If the explained variable is categorical, the analysis is called a classification analysis. If the explained variable is numerical, the analysis is called a regression analysis. Both of them are shortly named as CART analyses. CART is an abbreviation for Classification and Regression Tree analysis, used as an umbrella term for the two different kinds of decision tree analyses.

Before I move onto the next section on decision trees and random forests, I want to talk a little bit about the jargon that is specific to CART analysis. In our example, the 'gender' variable sits at the top of the decision tree. Gender is therefore known as the root of the tree. This root then forks into two paths as 'woman' and 'man,' i.e. possible gender values. These two paths are known as the branches. Similarly, these branches fork into two as well, 'old' and 'young.' 'Age' class, which stands in between the branches, is a node in this example. The outcomes or payoffs are the various t-shirt styles, and they are called the leaves (of the tree). In this example, all the leaves are different. However, some paths could lead to the same outcomes. For example, there would be nothing wrong if we concluded that both the young female and young male customers tend to choose v-neck t-shirts. Plus, the decision trees need not be symmetric. Some branches could be shorter, and that would be totally fine. Finally, our tree could be larger, of course. If there were other variables forming nodes below the age class, they would be called the children of age, while age – a node above the other nodes – would be their parent. Each sequence of nodes has a similar child–parent relationship, by the way.

Decision trees and random forests

In statistics and machine learning, a decision tree is basically a decision support tool. It is useful for producing all the conditional outcomes that one should consider before making a decision. Remember the t-shirt seller's example in the previous section. Suppose that we are about to place an order of 100 new t-shirts with our wholesaler. What kind of t-shirts should they be if we are planning to sell them in our store? The decision tree analysis tells us to look at the relevant factors affecting t-shirt demand for certain t-shirt styles. For instance, we have already identified that young male customers are more likely to purchase baseball style t-shirts, while old male customers are more likely to prefer a polo style, etc. If most of our customers are young males, everything else remaining the same, most of the t-shirts in our bulk order from the wholesaler must be baseball style t-shirts.

As a popularly used decision support tool by data scientists and statisticians, decision trees have several advantages and disadvantages at the same time. First of all, decision trees are simple tools. Anyone, without prior experience in statistics or data sciences, can easily understand the results. Plus, decision trees do not require much data observation. Although the greater the number of observations, the more reliable the outcomes are, decision trees can still be constructed with a minimal amount of observations, and non-numerical data such as expert opinions or personal experiences might be integrated into the analysis quite easily. These are the advantages of decision trees. As for the disadvantages, tree stability is an important problem since small changes in data often lead to large changes in the tree structures. Plus, information gain is usually biased toward those variables with more levels if categorical variables are used since the mutual dependence of categorical variables, i.e. a measure of mutual information between them, tends to be higher as the number of their levels increase. However, one could always use random forests instead of a decision tree in order to overcome this sort of robustness and stability issues.

When random forest methodology was first proposed in 1995 by Ho of Bell Laboratories, the idea that Ho put forward was simple. Decision trees trained over fixed datasets usually overfit to the training data. Pruning a fully-grown tree (eliminating some parts of the tree) might increase the prediction accuracy of our decisions over the testing data while decreasing the prediction accuracy on the training data. This trade-off can be thought of as a reflection of the usual bias-variance trade-off of predictions over the training dataset. However, when you prune a tree, you lose its complexity. In Ho's own words,

> apparently there is a fundamental limitation on the complexity of tree classifiers – they should not be grown too complex to overfit the training data. No method is known that can grow trees to arbitrary complexity, and increase both training and testing set accuracy at the same time.

Random forests have later proven themselves as the more robust and stable classifiers, so they have to be constructed rather than a single decision tree whenever the researcher has the chance to do so.

A random forest is nothing but a collection of decision trees whose predictions are aggregated into one final prediction. A random forest is called 'forest' for its being a collection of trees, but why is it random? It is random because it randomly chooses the independent variables that would be used to construct decision trees. Let us say that we have observations of 20 different variables, which might be explaining a single independent variable. A random forest would use only a subset of these 20 variables in each decision tree that it includes. For example, the forest would use four variables in each decision tree. Then every single tree would utilize four variables. Different trees would use different sets of four. If we grow a large number of decision trees, all of the 20 variables would be used eventually. If the selection of independent variables was not randomized, base trees in the forest could become highly correlated because a small number of variables out of the 20 could be particularly predictive and so they would be used in the construction of an overly large number of base trees.

Predicting the sign of exchange rates with a random forest

In Chapter 6, I compared the out-of-sample predictive powers of various structural and time series models with that of a random walk model and, unfortunately, in most of the cases, the random walk model has empirically proven itself as the best predictor of exchange rates. That finding was unfortunate, but not unexpected. The random walk has been reported by numerous studies as the champion model of exchange rate predictions since it was first announced as the best out-of-sample predictor by Meese and Rogoff in 1983. Since the superiority of random walk over the more complicated models has been repeatedly proven, changing our prediction strategy might be a good idea. The first question I want to raise in this book – if we are ever going to change our strategy – is whether we need to make point estimations. In my consideration, predicting the direction of change is useful enough in most cases for market participants and policymakers. Fund managers could decide on profitable portfolio mixes as long as they know that currency A will appreciate and currency B will depreciate, etc. They need to know more than this only in a limited number of cases, such as whether they are planning to sell options or make the net present value analysis of a project, etc.

If we are going to estimate the direction of change (i.e. the sign of change, which means estimating the change in the positive or negative direction) for the exchange rates, which methods should we use? My answer to this question would be to use a classifier. However, decision trees would not be suitable for their overfitting problems to the training data and instability issues. A better choice would be to use random forests. In order to grow a forest of decision trees, I use the following variables: i) exchange rate changes, ii) percentage growth rates of industrial production, iii) interest rates, and iv) money supply (m2 aggregate) growth rates. Those structural variables are the variables used in the monetary model of the exchange rate, a model we have discussed in this book in Chapter 2. Remember that the precise monetary model, which we have derived, was as follows:

$$\Delta s_{t+1} = \beta(y - y^*) - (m - m^*) + (p - p^*)$$

In this specification, $(y - y^*)$ was the GDP growth rate difference. In the following example, I have used the industrial production data instead of the GDP since GDP observations are not available on a monthly basis. For countries such as Japan and the US, industrial production can be used as a reliable proxy for the GDP. The second term, i.e. $(m - m^*)$, is the money supply difference. Similarly, the third term, i.e. $(p - p^*)$, is the inflation rate difference. Although the monetary model takes the differences of all these variables, I have used them individually in this random forest analysis, hoping that this would allow the random forest to capture more associations. Table 7.1 presents the prediction results (confusion matrices and the

Table 7.1 Random walk model prediction accuracy and the confusion matrix

	True category: 1	*True category: 0*
Predicted category: 1	29	28
Predicted category: 0	44	42
Prediction accuracy	49.65%	

Notes: Category 1 means the exchange rate has increased (+ sign)
        Category 2 means the exchange rate has decreased (− sign)

out-of-sample prediction accuracies) for the random forest and the random walk models.

The random walk model has an almost 50% prediction accuracy on the testing dataset of 143 observations (30% of the total observations were spared for testing). The random forest model, on the other hand, has 74% prediction accuracy on the same dataset (Table 7.2). Clearly, the winner of the sign prediction contest is the random forest model. The random walk model has a particularly bad performance in the estimation of category 1.

If we focus on the prediction accuracy of the random walk model, which is almost 50%, I believe that we can better understand how the random walk model does its predictions and so what it is that we need to surpass with alternative specifications in order to produce better prediction results.

Figure 7.2 is a histogram, which shows us the number of observations in each category.

As this histogram shows, the number of observations are split almost 50–50 between categories 0 and 1. The error term of the random walk model has a symmetric distribution around zero. Therefore, the random walk model is expected to make correct sign predictions 50% of the time. That is why, if there exist 73 observations of category 1 and 70 observations of category 0, as in our example, we should expect that the random walk model would guess category 1 correctly about 36 or 37 times and guess category 0 correctly about 35 times. In sum, we should expect the random walk model to make correct predictions around 71 or 72 times out of 143 attempts. As you must have seen, 71/143 = 0.4965, i.e. the prediction accuracy we have measured for the random walk model in this example. In sum, our random walk model seems to have delivered a prediction accuracy that is pretty much in line with expectations given the distributions of observations and the error term. In short, the random walk model has delivered us a best-guess statistical result, only dependent on the error term's distribution and the binary split of the categorical observations. The random forest model's

Table 7.2 Random forest model prediction accuracy and the confusion matrix

	True category: 1	*True category: 0*
Predicted category: 1	53	16
Predicted category: 0	21	53
Prediction accuracy	74.13%	

Notes: Category 1 means the exchange rate has increased (+ sign)
    Category 2 means the exchange rate has decreased (− sign)
    Number of trees grown is 300, number of variables at each split is six

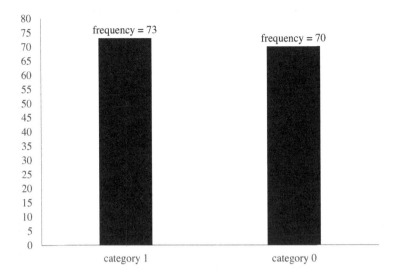

Figure 7.2 The split of the testing data among the two categories

prediction accuracy of 74% then means the random forest is able to extract 24% more useful information from the structural variables on top of the best-guess result. In my consideration, this is a significant improvement and a confirmation of the importance of the structural variables for predicting – at least – the sign of the exchange rates.

Following is the R code that I used for growing a random forest for the USD/JPY exchange rate as an example. The selection of the variables that I have used in the trees of the following random forest is based on the monetary model.

```
###############################################################
#                 CART ANALYSIS IN R:                        #
#                 RANDOM FOREST ESTIMATION                   #
###############################################################
# first, let us call the ggplot2 library, which we will need for
# plotting the trees at the end let us also call the randomForest
# library, which is one of the most useful libraries for doing
# random forest simulation

library(ggplot2)

library(randomForest)

# upload your data to R using the read.csv command
```

```
data = read.csv("RoutledgeBookRandomForestData.csv", header = TRUE)

data = data[,-1] # here we get rid of the first column, where we
                   have the dates

str(data)          # that shows us the structure of the variables,
                     i.e. if they are numeric or not, etc.


# we change the structure of the dependent variable from integer
  to factor down below
# (now our analysis will automatically be a classification
  analysis and not regression analysis)

data$USDJPYsign = as.factor(data$USDJPYsign)  # USDJPYsign is
the dependent variable

####################################
# In the preceding lines we checked the structure of the
# variables. I would like stop for a moment to explain the
# importance of checking the structure of the variables with
# the 'str' function before I share rest of the code. I will
# use an example for that explanation.
# Assume that we have a variable, x. Let x be a categorical
# variable. For example, x might be the number of stars a
# restaurant receives from its reviewers on the internet.
# Five star means highly satisfied customer, while one star
# means the opposite. Also assume that these stars are recorded
# numerically. That is to say, '1' is recorded if a one-star
# review is written for the.  restaurant, '2' is recorded if
# a 2-star review is written, so on and so forth. If these
# records are recognized by R as numerical entries, then the
# randomForest library would make a regression analysis
# although our data is indeed non-numerical and 1 only means 'so
# bad', 2 means 'bad',  . . . , 5 means 'so good' categorically.
# In such cases, we have to introduce the true structure of our
# data to R with a command as follows (assuming the name of our
# variable is 'reviews'.
#
# reviews = as.factor(reviews)
#
####################################

# data partitioning. We spare 90% of data for training, while
  remaining 10% reserved for testing

ind = sample(2, nrow(data), replace = TRUE, prob = c(0.9, 0.1))
train = data[ind==1,]
test = data[ind==2,]

# Random Forest
```

```
rf = randomForest(USDJPYsign~., data=train,
          ntree = 300,
          mtry = 6,
          importance = TRUE,
          proximity = TRUE)
print(rf)
attributes(rf)

# prediction and confusion matrix - for the training data

library(caret)
p1 = predict(rf, train)
confusionMatrix(p1, train$USDJPYsign)

# prediction and confusion matrix - for the testing data

p2 = predict(rf, test)
confusionMatrix(p2, test$USDJPYsign)

# error rate of Random Forest

plot(rf)

# Tune mtry
t = tuneRF(train[,-1], train[,1],
    stepFactor = 2,
    plot = TRUE,
    ntreeTry = 300,
    trace = TRUE,
    improve = 2)

# number of nodes for the trees

hist(treesize(rf),
    main = "No. of Nodes for the Trees",
    col = "green")

# variable importance

varImpPlot(rf,
      sort = TRUE,
      n.var = 9,
      main = "Top 9 - Variable Importance")
importance(rf)
varUsed(rf)

# partial dependence plot

partialPlot(rf, train, USm2, "2")
```

```
# extract single tree

getTree(rf, 1, labelVar = TRUE)

# multi-dimensional scaling plot of proximity matrix

MDSplot(rf, train$USDJPYsign)

# function for choosing random trees from random forest

library(dplyr)
library(ggraph)
library(igraph)

tree_func = function(rf,
             tree_num) {

# get tree by index

tree = randomForest::getTree(rf,
                    k = tree_num,
                    labelVar = TRUE) %>%
tibble::rownames_to_column() %>%
# make leaf split points to NA, so the 0s won't get plotted
mutate('split point' = ifelse(is.na(prediction), 'split point', NA))

# prepare data frame for graph

graph_frame <- data.frame(from = rep(tree$rowname, 2),
             to = c(tree$'left daughter', tree$'right
             daughter'))

# convert to graph and delete the last node that we don't want
to plot
graph <- graph_from_data_frame(graph_frame) %>%
  delete_vertices("0")

# set node labels
V(graph)$node_label <- gsub("_", " ", as.character(tree$'split var'))
V(graph)$leaf_label <- as.character(tree$prediction)
V(graph)$split <- as.character(round(tree$'split point', digits = 2))

# plot
plot <- ggraph(graph, 'dendrogram') +
  theme_bw() +
  geom_edge_link() +
  geom_node_point() +
  geom_node_text(aes(label = node_label), na.rm = TRUE, repel =
  TRUE) + geom_node_label(aes(label = split), vjust = 2.5,
```

```
  na.rm = TRUE, fill = "white") + geom_node_label(aes(label =
  leaf_label, fill = leaf_label), na.rm = TRUE,
                    repel = TRUE, colour = "white", fontface =
"bold", show.legend = FALSE) +
  theme(panel.grid.minor = element_blank(),
      panel.grid.major = element_blank(),
      panel.background = element_blank(),
      plot.background = element_rect(fill = "white"),
      panel.border = element_blank(),
      axis.line = element_blank(),
      axis.text.x = element_blank(),
      axis.text.y = element_blank(),
      axis.ticks = element_blank(),
      axis.title.x = element_blank(),
      axis.title.y = element_blank(),
      plot.title = element_text(size = 18))

  print(plot)
}

# tree with the minimum number of nods

library(labeling)

tree_num = which(rf$forest$ndbigtree == min(rf$forest$ndbigtree))
tree_func(rf = rf, tree_num)

# tree with the maximum number of nods

tree_num = which(rf$forest$ndbigtree == max(rf$forest$ndbigtree))
tree_func(rf = rf, tree_num)
############################# -O- #############################
```

8 Final remarks

The global foreign exchange market is the largest market in the world with its unparalleled volume of transactions. To be more precise, the transaction volume in the global foreign exchange market was recorded at $6.6 trillion a day on average by the BIS in 2019. If we roughly assume that there exist 250 business days in a typical year, the annual size of the market can be estimated as hovering around $1.65 quadrillion. In comparison, let us note that the outstanding market value of global bonds was $102.8 trillion and the total market capitalization of the global equity market was only $74.7 trillion in 2018. Quite shockingly though, an economic model that predicts the future exchange rates has yet to be introduced.

In 1983, Meese and Rogoff demonstrated the inability of the most prominent structural and time series models of the early 1980s, used to explain exchange rates, as useful predictive models. A driftless random walk model was able to beat all the structural and time series models with its superior out-of-sample prediction power. This was surely a very disappointing finding, given the fact that the random walk model is unpredictable itself. The random walk model is the discrete case counterpart of the continuous Brownian motion process, which is simply impossible to predict. Nevertheless, the unfortunate finding of Meese and Rogoff has since become one of the staples of exchange rate economics because although there have been myriad empirical attempts to overturn this gloomy finding since 1983, virtually all of them have failed. Given the last 40 years' account, the random walk model is still the undisputed champion of the exchange rate predictions. In plain English, in the last 40 years, the discipline of economics has been unsuccessful in finding a robust and reliable prediction model of exchange rates, and that is why we have to admit that we do not have a prediction model for the movements in the largest market in the world. This is not only a matter of disappointment, but it is also a scary fact given the size of the market and the possible consequences of sudden and totally unanticipated reversals in the exchange rates (Söylemez, 2013). Predicting the future exchange rates with acceptable accuracy would make the lives of investors and policymakers so much easier –if only they could.

In this book, I have revisited the exchange rate determination problem. My aim was to see whether recent improvements in statistics and data science could be used to make better exchange rate predictions. I have therefore employed a set of structural or purely time series models and tested their out-of-sample forecasting powers with unconventional specifications. My base model for the structural models was the linear Fama equation. I converted it into its regime-switching counterparts under different assumptions. I have also given a chance to linear models, but with unusual model selection criteria. As is well known, conventional statistics aims to estimate coefficients in an unbiased manner. However, empirical studies have proven so many times that a bias-variance trade-off (that is to say, allowing some bias in estimates in order to dampen the error variances) might provide us with better out-of-sample predictions since bias-variance trade-off prevents overfitting issues in the training dataset. The linear models that I used were Lasso, Ridge, and Elastic Net specifications of the Fama equation. All these different models were tested on real observations of the USD/JPY and USD/AUD exchange rates. According to the results, we can conclude the following points: i) using regime-switching models rather than a simple linear specification has helped us in improving the out-of-sample prediction power of the Fama equation; ii) however, the improvements are so minuscule – almost negligible; plus, iii) none of the models could have consistently surpassed the prediction results of the random walk. The datasets used in this book will be made available to researchers on request. The R codes that I have used in estimating the models or the screenshots of the Eviews program have already been provided to the readers.

Because the random walk model has once again proven its superiority over the structural and time series models as the better forecaster of exchange rates, regardless of the modifications I have introduced into the specification of the Fama equation, I have decided to question if it was possible to predict the direction of the changes in the exchange rates. Making better point estimations of the exchange rates than the random walk model seems to be a real challenge, but it could still be possible to beat the random walk predictions if we focus more on predicting the direction change rather than the exact exchange rate that would happen in the future. Moreover, predicting the direction of exchange rates is important information for many agents in financial markets. Fund managers could profit from a piece of information like this, while businesspeople could prevent losses and central bankers could design better forward-looking policies, etc. The precise methodologies I have chosen in this book for testing this idea were the decision trees and the random forest methodology. In fact, Chapter 7 is entirely dedicated to the introduction of these techniques. Also in Chapter 7, I compared the out-of-sample prediction capacity of a random forest model with that of the random walk. The random forest model in Chapter 7 was inspired by the monetary model of exchange rates in the selection of the structural variables. In the end, the random forest returned significantly better prediction results on the testing dataset. In Chapter 7, I also speculated on the possible reasons why a random forest model could surpass the random walk model with regard to its out-of-sample sign (direction) predictions. To wrap everything up, the discussions in this book indicate to us with utmost clarity the difficulty of making good exchange rate predictions. Even the latest statistical and data science techniques are prone to fail in one-to-one comparison against the random walk. However, there is a good chance that we can improve our prediction accuracy radically if we focus on making predictions on the possible direction of the future exchange rates rather than making point estimations.

Bibliography

Ahmad, Yamin & Stuart Glosser, 2007, Searching for Nonlinearities in Real Exchange Rates, Working Paper 09-01, UW-Whitewater, Department of Economics.

Baillie, Richard T. & Tim Bollerslev, 1994, Cointegration, Fractional Cointegration, and Exchange Rate Dynamics, *Journal of Finance*, American Finance Association, Vol. 49(2), 737–745.

Baillie, Richard T. & Rehim Kilic, 2006, Do Asymmetric and Nonlinear Adjustments Explain the Forward Premium Anomaly?, *Journal of International Money and Finance*, Elsevier, Vol. 25(1), 22–47.

Bansal, Ravi & Magnus Dahlquist, 2000, The Forward Premium Puzzle: Different Tales from Developed and Emerging Economies, *Journal of International Economics*, Vol. 51, 115–144.

Bilson, John F.O., 1978, Rational Expectations and the Exchange Rate, in: J. Frenkel & H. Johnson (eds.), *The Economics of Exchange Rates*, Reading: Addison-Wesley Press.

Bilson, John F.O., 1979, The Deutsche Mark/Dollar Rate: A Monetary Analysis, in: Karl Brunner & Allan H. Meltzer (eds.), *Policies for Employment, Prices and Exchange Rates*, Carnegie-Rochester Conference 11, Amsterdam: North-Holland Publishing Company.

Bilson, John F.O., 1981, The 'Speculative Efficiency' Hypothesis, *Journal of Business*, Vol. 54, 435–451.

Chaboud, Alain P. & Jonathan H. Wright, 2003, Uncovered Interest Parity: It Works, But Not For Long, International Finance Discussion Papers 752, Board of Governors of the Federal Reserve System, U.S.

Chinn, Menzie D. & Guy Meredith, 2005, Testing Uncovered Interest Parity at Short and Long Horizons during the Post-Bretton Woods Era, NBER Working Papers 11077, National Bureau of Economic Research, Inc.

Davidson, Russell & James G. MacKinnon, 1993, *Estimation and Inference in Econometrics*, New York: Oxford Press.

De Grauwe, Paul & Hans Dewahter, 1993, Chaos in the Dornbusch Model: The Role of Fundamentalists and Chartists, *Open Economies Review*, Vol. 4, 351–379.

Dornbusch, Rudiger, 1976, Expectations and Exchange Rate Dynamics, *Journal of Political Economy*, Vol. 84, 1161–1176.

Engel, Charles, 1996, The Forward Discount Anomaly and the Risk Premium: A Survey of Recent Evidence, NBER Working Papers 5312, National Bureau of Economic Research, Inc.

Fama, Eugene F., 1984, Forward and Spot Exchange Rates, *Journal of Monetary Economics*, Vol. 14(3), 319–338.

Foreign Exchange Markets, 30 June 2008, Chapter 5 of the Bank of International Settlements' 78th Annual Report. URL Link: www.bis.org/publ/arpdf/ar2008e. htm (Last accessed: 28.08.2020).

Frankel, Jeffrey A., 1979, On the Mark: A Theory of Floating Exchange Rates Based on Real Interest Differentials, *American Economic Review*, Vol. 69, 610–622.

Frenkel, Jacob A., 1976, A Monetary Approach to Exchange Rate: Doctrinal Aspects and Empirical Evidence, *Scandinavian Journal of Economics*, Vol. 78, 200–224.

Froot, A. Kenneth & Richard H. Thaler, 1990, Anomalies: Foreign Exchange, *The Journal of Economic Perspectives*, Vol. 4(3), 179–192.

Gupta, Prashant, 5 June 2017, Cross-Validation in Machine Learning. Article on the Towardsdatascience.com Webpage. URL Link: https://towardsdatascience.com/cross-validation-in-machine-learning-72924a69872f (Last accessed: 08.24.2020).

Ho, Tin K., 1995, Random Decision Forests, ICDAR '95: Proceedings of the Third International Conference on Document Analysis and Recognition, (Vol.1) – August.

Hooper, Peter & John E. Morton, 1982, Fluctuations in the Dollar: A Model of Nominal and Real Exchange Rate Determination, *Journal of International Money and Finance*, Vol. 1, 39–56.

IMF and the World Trade Organization, 13 March 2020, Article on the IMF Webpage. URL Link: www.imf.org/en/About/Factsheets/The-IMF-and-the-World-Trade-Organization (Last accessed: 08.28.2020).

Johansson, Martin, 2001, TAR Models and Real Exchange Rates, Working Papers 2001:21, Lund University, Department of Economics.

Kilian, Lutz & Mark P. Taylor, 2003, Why Is It So Difficult to Beat the Random Walk Forecast of Exchange Rates?, *Journal of International Economics*, Elsevier, Vol. 60(1), 85–107.

Meese, Richard A. & Kenneth Rogoff, 1983, Empirical Exchange Rate Models of the Seventies: Do They Fit Out of Sample?, *Journal of International Economics*, Vol. 14, 3–24.

Mussa, Michael, 1982, A Model of Exchange Rate Dynamics, *Journal of Political Economy*, Vol. 90(1), 74–104.

O'neal, John R., Frances H. Oneal, Zeev Maoz & Bruce Russett, 1996, The Liberal Peace: Interdependence, Democracy, and International Conflict, 1950–85, *Journal of Peace Research*, Vol. 33(1), 11–28.

Panos, Michael, A. Robert Nobay & David A. Peel, 1997, Transactions Costs and Nonlinear Adjustment in Real Exchange Rates: An Empirical Investigation, *Journal of Political Economy*, University of Chicago Press, Vol. 105(4), 862–879.

Pippenger, Michael & Gregory Goering, 1998, Exchange Rate Forecasting: Results from a Threshold Autoregressive Model, *Open Economies Review*, Springer, Vol. 9(2), 157–170.

Serletis, Apostolos & Asghar Shahmoradi, 2004, Absence of Chaos and 1/f Spectra, but Evidence of TAR Nonlinearities in the Canadian Exchange Rate, *Macroeconomic Dynamics*, Cambridge University Press, Vol. 8(4).

Söylemez, Arif O., 2013, Exchange Rate Misalignment in Turkey: Overvaluation of the Turkish Lira, *International Journal of Academic Research in Business and Social Sciences*, Vol. 3(4), 198–206.

Strikholm, Birgit & Timo Terasvirta, 2005, Determining the Number of Regimes in a Threshold Autoregressive Model Using Smooth Transition Autoregressions, Working Paper Series in Economics and Finance 578, Stockholm School of Economics, revised 11 Feb.

Terasvirta, Timo, 2004, Smooth Transition Regression Modelling, in: Helmut Lütkepohl & Markus Krätzig (eds.), *Applied Time Series Econometrics*, Cambridge, UK: Cambridge University Press.

US Environmental Protection Agency, 2010, CADDIS Volume 4: Basic Analyses / Additional Information on Classification and Regression Tree (CART) Analysis, Webpage content. www.epa.gov/caddis-volume-4-data-analysis-classification-and-regression-tree-cart-analysis (Last accessed: 28.08.2020).

Vandrovych, Vitaliy, 2006, *Nonlinearities in Exchange-Rate Dynamics: Chaos?*, State Street Global Advisors, Advanced Research Center.

Westerhoff, Frank, 2009, Exchange Rate Dynamics: A Nonlinear Survey, in: J.B. Rosser, Jr. (eds.), *Handbook of Research on Complexity*, Cheltenham: Edward Elgar.

Index

Printed in the United States
by Baker & Taylor Publisher Services